MARY BERRY'S

Simple Cakes

MARY BERRY'S
Simple Cakes

DELICIOUS STEP-BY-STEP RECIPES

BBC
BOOKS

Dedication

For Abby and Grace, our twin granddaughters. What joy they have brought to us all.
May they grow up to enjoy creating and cooking as much as their doting granny!

9 10

This edition published in 2014 by BBC Books, an imprint of Ebury Publishing.
A Random House Group Company.

First published in hardback as Foolproof Cakes in 2004.
Paperback edition published as Simple Cakes in 2006.
This edition first published in 2014.
Copyright © Mary Berry 2004, 2014
Food Photography © Jean Cazals 2004

The Random House Group Limited Reg. No. 954009

Addresses for companies within the Random House Group can be found at
www.randomhouse.co.uk

A CIP catalogue record for this book is available from the British Library.

ISBN: 9781849906807

Penguin Random House is committed to a sustainable future
for our business, our readers and our planet. This book is made
from Forest Stewardship Council® certified paper.

Printed and bound by Firmengruppe APPL, aprinta druck, Wemding, Germany

www.penguin.co.uk

Contents

Introduction

There really is nothing to beat a good home-made cake. There is no mystique about making them. You simply need to follow a good, sound recipe meticulously, use the very best ingredients, bake it in the right-sized tin at the advised oven temperature and then enjoy the result. In this book I have chosen the most popular classics, plus a few of my own favourites, and given step-by-step instructions for success with all of them.

Baking is a very straightforward science. The most important thing is to weigh out the ingredients accurately: 50 grams more flour in a cake would make it heavy and dry – unlike a soup or casserole, for example, where a few extra grams of meat or vegetables would not make any difference to the end result. I am often told by people that their granny made the best cakes they had ever tasted but she never weighed anything. However, when you stop to think about it, in the past there wasn't the choice we have now and most likely she only ever made a Victoria sandwich and a fruit cake, using the same tablespoon and cup to measure the ingredients every time. So even if she didn't weigh the ingredients she had an accurate system of measuring, and the recipes were probably handed down to her with the very same spoon and cup!

Fortunately, things are much easier in the kitchen nowadays. Not only do we have accurate scales but most of us also have electric mixers and food processors, so cake making is a doddle.

Cakes aren't just for teatime. Many of the cakes in this book can double up as dessert – for example, Lemon Meringue Roulade (see page 104), Blueberry and Summer Fruit Cheesecake (see page 116) and Pecan Pie (see page 106). I've included a good selection of biscuits, too, which can be served with ice creams and creamy desserts, added to a lunchbox, or simply enjoyed as a snack at any time of day.

I'm often asked how I manage to eat all these delicious cakes without becoming huge. The answer is to have a small slice, and not too often. Enjoy cakes in moderation, with family and friends, and you won't find the pounds piling on.

Cake-making Methods

All-in-one method

This is so simple and, to my mind, the easiest and best method for most cakes, traybakes and Victoria sandwiches. Simply measure all the ingredients into a large mixing bowl – I usually put the eggs in first and the rest of the ingredients on top. If butter or margarine is being used, it must be soft, at room temperature, so that it blends in easily with the rest of the ingredients. You can soften it in a microwave, if necessary, but take great care. It should be just soft, not overheated and oily. Beat for a short time, just until the ingredients are mixed – this can be done with a hand-held electric mixer, a free-standing mixer or in a food processor. Don't overbeat, otherwise the cake will be close-textured. As the beating time is so short, a little baking powder is added to the mixture in most recipes, even if self-raising flour is being used, to give extra rise.

Creaming

This is beating the fat (usually butter or margarine) and sugar together at room temperature until light and fluffy, then beating in the eggs and lastly folding in the flour by hand. I rarely use this method now, as I get quicker and consistently better results with the all-in-one method.

Whisking

Most whisked cakes contain no fat, and are therefore known as fatless sponges. The Black Cherry Swiss Roll on page 64 is made by this method. The eggs and sugar are whisked together with an electric whisk (or by hand) until the mixture is thick and has greatly increased in volume. It should be thick enough to leave a trail on the surface of the mixture in the bowl when drizzled from the whisk. The flour is then carefully folded into the mixture with a plastic spatula or a large metal spoon. I was taught to use plain flour for fatless sponges but I find self-raising is better and foolproof.

Rubbing in

I've only used the rubbing-in method for scones and pastry in this book. The fat is diced and then rubbed into the flour with your fingertips, or with a food processor or electric mixer, until the resulting mixture looks like a crumble.

Melting

Traditionally this simple method is used for gingerbread (see Classic Sticky Gingerbread on page 76). Usually golden syrup and/or treacle, sugar and fat are melted in a pan (it's important not to overheat them), then added to the other ingredients and mixed together. The mixture is then poured into the tin and baked.

Making pastry

Pastry can be made by hand or in a food processor. Be sure to have the fat at room temperature so it is easy to rub in. Most flan cases are 'baked blind' before the filling is added, otherwise the pastry would not be cooked in the time it takes to cook the filling. To bake blind, prick the base of the uncooked flan case with a fork and line it with baking parchment. Fill with baking beans or rice to weigh it down and then bake in a pre-heated oven until the pastry is nearly cooked. Remove the beans and baking parchment and return the pastry to the oven for 5–10 minutes to dry out. The cooked pastry case is now ready for the filling.

Ingredients and Equipment

INGREDIENTS

Below is a guide to the ingredients used in this book. Always buy the very best you can afford, and keep an eye on the use-by dates on dry ingredients such as flour and baking powder – they don't keep indefinitely.

Baking powder

Baking powder is a mixture of bicarbonate of soda and an acid powder, usually cream of tartar, plus a starch filler such as cornflour or rice flour. It is used when you need extra raising agent in a plainer cake mixture (e.g. scones) and with self-raising flour for the all-in-one method. In some recipes, such as gingerbread and some American and Canadian cakes, bicarbonate of soda is used on its own.

Bought pastry

I never make puff pastry and if I am in a hurry I might buy shortcrust or sweet pastry, too.

Butter

Butter is the best fat to use for baking when you can really taste the flavour. For shortbread it is a must. If using it for the all-in-one or creaming method, it should be at room temperature. I love to use unsalted butter for baking, although it is more expensive than salted. To get butter to room temperature when taking it straight from the fridge, microwave it for a few seconds, until soft but not oily.

Chocolate

Cocoa powder gives a true chocolate flavour in most cakes, but avoid the sweetened cocoa used for milk drinks. I like to 'cook' the cocoa powder in most recipes by mixing it to a paste with a little boiling water before adding it to

Clockwise from top: dark chocolate, almond extract, vanilla extract

the other ingredients. If a recipe calls for plain chocolate, I use Bournville and melt it slowly. Remember, chocolate can melt in a child's pocket so only a little heat is needed! Milk chocolate is difficult to melt and does not give a good flavour in cakes. When using white chocolate, buy a good-quality Continental one and take care when melting – if it gets too hot it will become grainy. Pure chocolate chips in white and dark chocolate are easy to melt and good to use in recipes.

Dried fruit

The dried fruits I use most in baking are sultanas, currants, raisins, apricots and cherries.

Clockwise from top: currants, pecans, almonds, walnuts, mixed fruits, apricots and candied peel (centre)

I am not a fan of candied peel and angelica. Most fruit now comes ready washed. It can dry out in the packet, once opened, so rewrap it in another polythene bag. If you know that you will not be making fruit cakes for some time and have dried fruit in the cupboard, freeze it in the polythene bag and it will keep for a couple of years.

Eggs

Large eggs are used for all the recipes in this book. For most recipes, and especially meringues, they should be at room temperature, as they then give a greater volume when beaten. If storing separated eggs in the fridge, keep the whites in a container covered with cling film and write in marker pen on the cling film the number of whites in the pot. They should keep for a week. Leftover yolks need to be kept in a small container. Spoon over a little cold water to prevent a skin forming on the yolks, then cover with cling film and write the number of yolks in the pot on the cling film. Use yolks for lemon curd or for caramel custard or crème brûlée.

Extracts and flavourings

Vanilla and almond extracts are stronger and far more authentic than essences. I avoid flavourings such as lemon or orange in bottles, preferring to use fresh lemons and oranges.

Flours

Most of the recipes for cakes in this book use self-raising flour. Plain flour is used mainly for pastry. In an emergency, you can use self-raising flour for everything. I rarely sift flour, although I do for fatless sponges made by the whisking method, as it combines with the eggs and sugar more easily. I also sift the flour to remove any lumps if there are other dry ingredients with it, such as cocoa powder or spices. Some supermarkets sell a soft cake flour but I have not suggested using it as it can be difficult to find and I have always had success with self-raising flour. Wholemeal flour gives a closer texture and nutty flavour. For cakes and scones, I find it best to use a self-raising wholemeal flour.

Clockwise from top: flour, puff pastry and baking powder

Clockwise from top left: egg, butter and margarine

Margarine

Margarine is very good for baking and the flavours have greatly improved over recent years. However, many of the baking margarines in tubs, such as Blueband and Stork SB, have disappeared from the supermarkets now, and you have to be sure you are buying a margarine and not a spread. It is easy to confuse the two, since they are packaged in a similar way. All the spreads contain a higher proportion of water and less fat than margarine and butter. The brand name is on top and the word 'spread' often appears on the bottom of the tub in small letters. When baking, you need fat in order to keep a cake moist, and if you use a spread that has had water added – some of them contain as much as 50 per cent – it will affect the keeping quality of the cake and the results will not be as good.

Nuts

Keen bakers use whole, flaked and ground almonds, plus walnuts, pecans and more. I always keep nuts in the freezer in one big bag, each type in its own small bag. Whole nuts keep for years well wrapped and frozen and you know that they will taste fresh. They go rancid after a few months on the larder or kitchen shelf.

Oil

Some American and Canadian cake recipes – carrot cake, for example – use oil instead of butter or margarine. Only use vegetable, sunflower or nut oil, not olive oil, which is far too strong in flavour.

Sugars and sweeteners

I use unrefined caster sugar, golden granulated, light and dark muscovado, and demerara sugar in the recipes in this book. White caster sugar is finer than granulated and therefore perfect for cakes. Some brown sugars have added colouring, so I prefer to use natural brown sugar, which is always stated on the label. When muscovado sugar becomes hard in the packet through long storage, microwave it for a few moments to separate the grains. Icing sugar is best for icing and dusting over cakes to give an attractive finish.

Golden syrup, black treacle, maple syrup and honey are also good to have on the larder shelf for cake making.

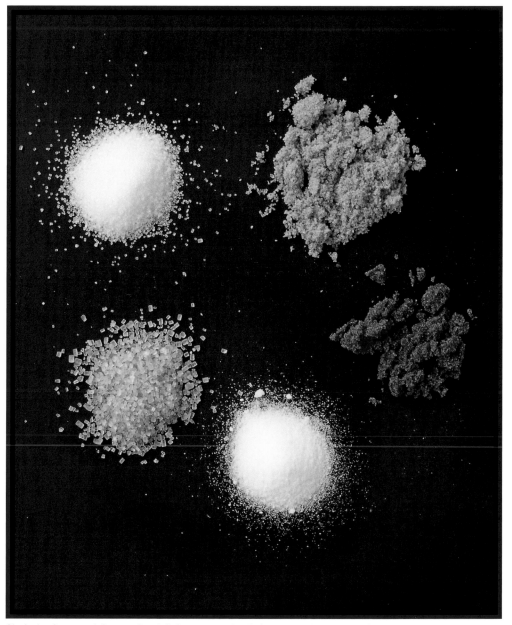

Clockwise from top left: granulated, light muscovado, dark muscovado, caster and demerara sugars

EQUIPMENT

I keep my baking equipment to a minimum – below is a list of the items I use most frequently.

Bowls

A set of Pyrex or Duralux bowls that fit one inside the other takes up less room in the cupboard. An extra, really large bowl is handy for making a celebration cake or a large amount of any mixture. Failing this, use a clean washing-up bowl or a large preserving pan.

Cake tins

Always choose good, solid cake tins. Use non-stick ones if you like, but I always grease cake and sandwich tins, then line the base with a disc of non-stick baking parchment for cakes such as Victoria sandwich, cherry and light fruit cakes. When making rich celebration cakes, I line the sides as well, so it doesn't matter whether the tin is non-stick or not. Then you can easily remove the cake from the tin. I prefer to use non-stick muffin and bun tins because you do not need to line them before putting the mixture in.

I've always washed my tins rather than just wiping them after use. The important thing is to dry them well and store in a dry cupboard to prevent them going rusty.

See page 20 for more about lining cake tins.

Tins used in this book
• loose-bottomed, deep, round 18 cm (7 in) cake tin
• loose-bottomed, deep, round 20 cm (8 in) cake tin
• loose-bottomed, deep, round 23 cm (9 in) cake tin
• two loose-bottomed 20 cm (8 in) sandwich tins, 4 cm (1½ in deep)
• loose-bottomed 23 cm (9 in) fluted flan tin
• 900 g (2 lb) loaf tin, 17 x 9 x 9 cm (6½ x 3½ x 3½ in) base measurement
• 30 x 23 x 4 cm (12 x 9 x 1½ in) traybake or roasting tin
• 33 x 23 cm (13 x 9 in) Swiss roll tin
• three baking trays
• deep 12-hole muffin tin
• two 12-hole mini-muffin tins

Additional tins

You might like to have the following tins for other recipes or for baking small quantities:

• two 450 g (1 lb) loaf tins instead of one 900 g (2 lb) tin – perhaps to make one cake to eat straight away and one to freeze
• two 18 cm (7 in) sandwich tins for a three-egg quantity instead of four
• two 12-hole bun tins for mince pies
• 20 cm (8 in) and 23 cm (9 in) springform tins to use for cheesecakes, Key Lime Pie and Banoffi Pie, if preferred

Flexible plastic spatula

This is used to get every last bit of mixture out of the bowl. The white ones are best, but avoid putting them in the dishwasher as they eventually become sticky.

Food processor

A food processor is handy for rubbing-in mixtures, making pastry, bread and batters and chopping nuts. It is not suitable for making meringues, as the bowl is enclosed and does not hold enough air to give the meringue volume.

Take care when using a food processor for making cakes. They are extremely fast and mix the ingredients in moments, so watch like a hawk and stop the machine the minute the mixture has combined, as overbeating means the cake will be too close-textured once baked.

Free-standing electric mixer

Keen bakers would not be without one of these. They usually have a whisk for cake making and meringues, and a dough hook for kneading bread. They have the great advantage that while they are mixing you are free to do something else. The disadvantage is that they take up space on the worktop. I keep mine on a rise-and-fall shelf in a cupboard below the worktop, which I lift out to use the machine, then tuck away again afterwards.

Hand-held electric whisk

One of the most frequently used pieces of equipment in my kitchen. Hand-held electric

Above, left to right: roasting tin with rack, baking sheet, Swiss roll tin and loose-bottomed fluted flan tin

Clockwise from top: balloon whisk, flat spatula, measuring spoons, timer, rectangular wire cooling rack, palette knife, muffin tray and piping bag

whisks are surprisingly reasonable in price and very quick and efficient to use. When beating egg whites for meringues, always choose a large bowl and move the whisk all over the base to incorporate as much air as possible.

Measuring jug

Glass measuring jugs are best, as you can see at a glance the level marked on the side. Always stand the jug on a flat surface rather than holding it in the air at eye level.

Measuring spoons

A set of spoons from 2.5 ml (½ teaspoon) to 15 ml (1 tablespoon) is needed for measuring small amounts of liquids, flour and spices. When measuring dry ingredients, all spoonfuls should be level unless otherwise stated in the recipe.

Metal baking trays

Choose really thick, rigid, solid baking trays in the largest size that fits your oven. If you can, store them vertically in cupboards, as they take up less room that way.

Non-stick liners

Silicone non-stick baking parchment is excellent for lining cake tins and baking trays but you do have to throw it away after use. Baco Glide and Lift Off paper, which is thicker and longer lasting, are both very good to use as a liner; simply wash and use again and again. The sheets can be cut to fit the base of cake tins, Swiss roll tins and baking trays.

Nylon piping bag

If you are in a hurry, it is perfectly all right to shape meringues in blobs with a spoon rather than piping them. However, you do need a piping bag for éclairs. Smaller bags are useful to pipe icing. The advantage of nylon piping bags is that they can be rinsed and then washed in the washing machine. I use a 1 cm (½ in) plain nozzle for piping meringues and éclairs and a rose nozzle for piping cream – both plastic and metal are good to use.

Oven

Ovens can vary considerably, whether they are gas, electric or fan assisted. Fan-assisted ovens cook more quickly, so you need to reduce the temperature by about 20°C (check with your oven handbook). The recipes for this book were tested in a conventional electric oven. I thoroughly recommend buying an oven thermometer if you are a keen baker, then you can be exact. Put the thermometer on the centre shelf of the oven when it is set at the temperature you require and adjust the setting accordingly.

Don't open the door of the oven once the cake is baking. Wait until halfway through the cooking time, or look through the glass door, then gently open the door and check how it is doing. If the cake is getting a little darker than you would like but is not yet cooked through, cover it loosely with foil. Make a note on the recipe to cook it at a slightly lower temperature next time.

Baking in an Aga is easy once you've mastered the technique. Refer to the book that comes free with the Aga, or write to Aga Rayburn, PO Box 30, Ketley, Telford, Shropshire TF1 4DD (www.agarayburn.co.uk).

Palette knife

These should be bendy and flexible, one large and one small. Use for spreading icing and other mixtures. The large one is handy for lifting biscuits off baking trays once cooked.

Pastry utensils

Rolling pin
A wooden rolling pin without handles is the most practical. If all else fails, you can use a glass milk bottle!

Pastry brush
Instead of buying pastry brushes, buy a good untreated paintbrush, about 5 cm (2 in) wide. This is usually better and cheaper than a pastry brush.

Plain and fluted cutters
These are used to cut out scones and biscuits. The best are made of metal and are fluted at one end, plain at the other (these are often

Clockwise from top: balance scales, baking parchment, electric hand whisk and glass mixing bowls

Clockwise from bottom left: wooden spoon, sieve, measuring jug, rolling pin, pastry brush, circular wire cooling rack, metal skewer, sponge sandwich tin and metal cutters sold in sets in tins). Before cutting out, always dunk the cutter in flour so the mixture won't stick. If you don't have any cutters, use an appropriate-sized glass (upside down) instead.

Scales

The most vital piece of equipment. You cannot make successful cakes without them. I prefer balance scales, i.e. with weights on one side and the scale pan on the other. These are accurate to 5 grams, providing you've levelled them up to start with. It is easy to update from Imperial simply by buying a set of metric weights.

Electronic scales can be temperamental just before the battery runs out. Spring-balanced scales are often not accurate with small amounts. You can always check your scales for accuracy by putting an unopened bag of sugar or coffee (or anything else with the weight written on the packet) on them.

Sieve

Choose strong, stainless-steel sieves that are dishwasher-proof.

Skewers

Long, thin metal skewers are useful for testing when a cake is done. Gently pierce the centre of the cake when you expect it to be cooked. If the skewer comes out clean with no mixture on it, the cake is ready.

Timers

It is a great help to set a kitchen timer when baking. Don't rely on checking the clock every few minutes.

Whisk

A balloon whisk with plenty of wires is useful for whisking eggs and small amounts of mixture but now I always prefer to use an electric whisk.

Wire cooling rack

Once cakes and biscuits come out of the oven, they should be cooled on a wire rack. These can be round or rectangular. If you don't have

one, you could use the rack from the grill pan or roasting tray.

Wooden spoons

I rarely use a bowl-shaped wooden spoon. I much prefer the flat spatula-shaped ones – so easy to scrape off the mixture. I have flat-ended ones to get to the corners of pans and round-ended ones for beating mixture in bowls.

USEFUL INFORMATION
Lining cake tins

To line a round, deep Christmas cake tin (23 cm/9 in)
Cut a strip of non-stick baking parchment to fit twice around the sides of the tin. Fold the bottom edge of the strip up by about 2.5 cm (1 in), creasing it firmly, then open out the fold and cut slanting lines into this narrow strip at intervals. Put a circle of non-stick baking parchment into the base of the tin, lightly grease the outer edge and then fit the prepared strip of parchment with the snipped edge in the base of the tin to line the sides. Place a second circle of non-stick baking parchment in the tin to cover the cut part of the paper (see also page 78).

To line a Swiss roll tin (33 x 23 cm/13 x 9 in)
Place the tin on top of the baking parchment and cut a rectangle approximately 5 cm (2 in) bigger than the tin all round. Grease the tin and then press the paper inside. To square off, make a snip in each corner of the paper down to the corner of the tin, then secure the corners together with a paper clip.

To line a large loaf tin (900 g/2 lb)
Cut a piece of baking parchment to fit up the wide sides and over the base of the tin. Grease the tin and press the paper into place. You do not need to line the ends of the tin – simply loosen the cake with a palette knife before removing.

To line a traybake or roasting tin (30 x 23 x 4 cm/12 x 9 x 1½ in)
For all the traybake recipes in this book you

Above: lined tins

can line the tin with either baking parchment or aluminium foil; the foil provides a handy way of storing the cake after baking. To line with foil, turn the tin over and mould a large piece of foil over the base. Then simply flip the tin over again and place the moulded foil inside – grease before using. To line with non-stick baking parchment, cut a rectangle of baking parchment to fit the tin. Grease the tin and then line with the paper. To square off, make a snip in each corner of the paper down to the corner of the tin, then secure the corners together with a paper clip.

Storing cakes

Cakes can be stored in an airtight tin or plastic container. If they have a filling or icing of fresh cream, they should be kept in the fridge. It is essential to store biscuits in an airtight container to prevent them becoming soggy. They are often improved by refreshing in a moderate oven for 5–10 minutes, then cooled and enjoyed.

Freezing cakes

Most cakes freeze well. It is often useful to freeze them wrapped and un-iced, then thaw and ice them later. This way they take up less room in the freezer. If a cake is decorated, place it on a cardboard plate, freeze for about 10 hours, until solid, then carefully wrap it and return to the freezer, placing it where it won't get knocked. Alternatively, transfer it to a poly-thene cake box for protection, then put it back in the freezer.

Scones freeze brilliantly but, like biscuits, are greatly improved once thawed by refreshing in a moderate oven for 5–10 minutes. Cool and serve lukewarm.

Secrets of success

- Use large eggs for all the recipes in this book.

- Weigh the ingredients out carefully and accu-rately in either metric or Imperial, but don't mix the two.

- Pre-heat the oven before use. The pre-heating time will vary – check with the manufacturer's instruction book, if you still have it. As a general rule, conventional electric ovens take about 30 minutes, gas and fan ovens about 10 minutes.

- Mix the cake following the recipe instructions and place in the correct-sized tin.

- Bake on the shelf in the centre of the oven. If your oven cooks more quickly at the sides and back, carefully turn the tin or tray round towards the end of the cooking time, once the cake has set.

Testing for doneness

- Cakes should look cooked and an even colour, according to type.

- Sponges should shrink from the side of the tin and spring back when lightly touched with the fingertips.

- Fruit cakes and large cakes should be tested by inserting a fine skewer, which should come out clean.

- Biscuits should be evenly baked and lightly coloured underneath.

What went wrong?

- **Cake cracks on top**
  The oven was too hot or the cake placed on too high a shelf in the oven. The cake forms a crust too quickly, then the mixture continues to rise and the crust cracks.

- **Fruit sinks to the bottom of the cake**
  The mixture was too runny to support the fruit, or the fruit was wet or, in the case of cherries, sticky and coated in a heavy syrup. Always cut cherries in half or into quarters, then wash in a sieve and dry thoroughly on kitchen paper.

- **Cake sinks**
  The cake was taken out of the oven before it was done, so it sinks as it cools. Too much baking powder was used so it rose in the oven at the beginning, then collapsed at the

end of the cooking time. The oven door was opened before the cake was set.

• Cake does not rise properly
The mixture was overbeaten so the air was beaten out. Not enough raising agent or no raising agent was added. The oven was too cool. Whisked sponges were insufficiently whisked or over-mixed when adding the flour.

• Spots on the surface of the cake
Granulated sugar was used instead of caster, or demerara used instead of light muscovado (both granulated and demerara are coarse sugars).

• Cake is dry
The fat was not measured correctly. The cake was in the oven too long. Insufficiently wrapped once cooked and cooled.

Conversion tables

Conversions are approximate and have been rounded up or down. Follow one set of measurements only – do not mix metric and Imperial.

Weights		Volume		Measurements	
Metric	Imperial	Metric	Imperial	Metric	Imperial
15 g	½ oz	25 ml	1 fl oz	0.5 cm	¼ inch
25 g	1 oz	50 ml	2 fl oz	1 cm	½ inch
40 g	1½ oz	85 ml	3 fl oz	2.5 cm	1 inch
50 g	2 oz	150 ml	5 fl oz (¼ pint)	5 cm	2 inches
75 g	3 oz	300 ml	10 fl oz (½ pint)	7.5 cm	3 inches
100 g	4 oz	450 ml	15 fl oz (¾ pint)	10 cm	4 inches
150 g	5 oz	600 ml	1 pint	15 cm	6 inches
175 g	6 oz	700 ml	1¼ pints	18 cm	7 inches
200 g	7 oz	900 ml	1½ pints	20 cm	8 inches
225 g	8 oz	1 litres	1¾ pints	23 cm	9 inches
250 g	9 oz	1.2 litres	2 pints	25 cm	10 inches
275 g	10 oz	1.25 litres	2¼ pints	30 cm	12 inches
350 g	12 oz	1.5 litres	2½ pints		
375 g	13 oz	1.6 litres	2¾ pints	**Oven temperatures**		
400 g	14 oz	1.75 litres	3 pints	140°C	275°F	Gas Mk 1
425 g	15 oz	1.8 litres	3¼ pints	150°C	300°F	Gas Mk 2
450 g	1 lb	2 litres	3½ pints	160°C	325°F	Gas Mk 3
550 g	1¼ lb	2.1 litres	3¾ pints	180°C	350°F	Gas Mk 4
675 g	1½ lb	2.25 litres	4 pints	190°C	375°F	Gas Mk 5
900 g	2 lb	2.75 litres	5 pints	200°C	400°F	Gas Mk 6
1.5 kg	3 lb	3.4 litres	6 pints	220°C	425°F	Gas Mk 7
1.75 kg	4 lb	3.9 litres	7 pints	230°C	450°F	Gas Mk 8
2.25 kg	5 lb	5 litres	8 pints (1 gal)	240°C	475°F	Gas Mk 9

CHOCOLATE
CAKES

Sachertorte

A superb rich, very densely textured cake, named after the Sacher hotel in Vienna. Ground almonds replace the flour, which means this chocolate cake keeps well.

preparation time: 30 minutes
cooking time: 40–45 minutes
tin needed: a deep, round, loose-
   bottomed 23 cm (9 in) cake tin

265 g (9½ oz) plain chocolate, broken into pieces
6 eggs, 5 of them separated
215 g (7½ oz) caster sugar
150 g (5 oz) ground almonds

For the topping and icing:
about 4 tablespoons apricot jam
150 g (5 oz) plain chocolate, broken into pieces
150 ml (5 fl oz) double cream
25 g (1 oz) white chocolate

1 Lightly grease the cake tin and line the base with a circle of non-stick baking parchment. Pre-heat the oven to 180°C/350°F/Gas Mark 4. Put the chocolate into a bowl placed over a pan of hot water. The water in the pan must not touch the bowl or the chocolate may overheat. Place the pan over a low heat until the chocolate has melted, stirring occasionally. Allow to cool a little.

2 Whisk the 5 egg whites in a large mixing bowl until stiff but not dry. In a separate large mixing bowl, use a hand-held electric mixer to whisk together the 5 egg yolks, whole egg and sugar until thick and pale. The mixture should be thick enough to leave a trail on the surface when the whisk is lifted from the bowl.

3 Whisk the ground almonds, melted chocolate and 1 tablespoon of the whisked egg whites into the egg yolk mixture.

4 Carefully fold in the remaining egg whites using a large metal spoon or a straight-edged plastic spatula. Turn the mixture into the prepared tin and gently tilt the tin to level the surface. Bake for 40–45 minutes, until the crust that forms on the top is firm and the cake has begun to shrink away from the side of the tin.

5 Allow the cake to cool in the tin for about 10 minutes before loosening it around the edge with a small palette knife. Turn the cake upside down on to a wire rack covered with a tea towel, remove the lining paper and leave to cool completely.

6 For the topping, gently heat the apricot jam in a small pan and then brush it evenly over the top and sides of the cake (heating the jam makes it easier to brush).

7 For the icing, put the chocolate into a bowl with the double cream and melt slowly over a pan of hot water. Stir occasionally until smooth and glossy. Allow the icing to cool and thicken slightly, then pour it into the centre of the cake. Spread it gently over the top and down the sides with a palette knife and leave to set. To finish, melt the white chocolate slowly in a bowl over a pan of hot water. Spoon into a small paper icing bag or polythene bag and snip off the corner. Pipe 'Sacher' across the cake and leave to set.

Chocolate brownies

The best brownies are soft in the centre and have a crust on top. This recipe couldn't be simpler – all you do is measure the ingredients into a bowl and give it all a good mix!

preparation time: 15 minutes
cooking time: 40–45 minutes
tin needed: a traybake tin or
    roasting tin, 30 x 23 x 4 cm
    (12 x 9 x 1½ in)
makes 24

275 g (10 oz) margarine,
    softened
375 g (13 oz) caster sugar
4 eggs
75 g (3 oz) cocoa powder
100 g (4 oz) self-raising flour
100 g (4 oz) plain chocolate
    chips

1 Cut a rectangle of non-stick baking parchment to fit the base and sides of the tin. Grease the tin and then line it with the paper, pushing it neatly into the corners. Pre-heat the oven to 180°C/350°F/ Gas Mark 4. Measure all the ingredients into a large bowl and mix with a hand-held electric mixer until evenly blended.

2 Spoon the mixture into the prepared tin, scraping the sides of the bowl with a plas-tic spatula to remove all of it. Spread the mixture gently to the corners of the tin and level the top with the back of the spatula.

3 Bake for 40–45 minutes, until the brownies have a crusty top and a skewer inserted into the centre comes out clean. Cover loosely with foil for the last 10 minutes if the mixture is browning too much. Allow the brownies to cool in the tin and then cut into 24 squares. Store in an airtight tin.

Death by chocolate cake

I have given a generous amount of icing to fill and ice this cake, as death by chocolate should be sheer luxury and a complete indulgence! The icing is very easy to make, but take care not to overheat it or it will lose its shine. For the same reason, don't store the cake in the fridge – a cool place is fine.

preparation time: 40 minutes
cooking time: 35 minutes
tins needed: 2 loose-bottomed
  20 cm (8 in) sandwich tins,
  4 cm (1½ in) deep

275 g (10 oz) plain flour
3 tablespoons cocoa powder
1½ teaspoons bicarbonate of
  soda
1½ teaspoons baking powder
215 g (7½ oz) caster sugar
3 tablespoons golden syrup
3 eggs, beaten
225 ml (8 fl oz) sunflower oil
225 ml (8 fl oz) milk

For the icing:
450 g (1 lb) plain chocolate,
  broken into pieces
200 g (7 oz) unsalted butter

For the chocolate waves:
about 50 g (2 oz) each white
  and plain chocolate

1 Lightly grease the tins and line the bases with non-stick baking parchment. Pre-heat the oven to 160°C/325°F/Gas Mark 3. Sift the flour, cocoa powder, bicarbonate of soda and baking powder into a large bowl. Add the sugar and mix well.

2 Make a well in the centre of the dry ingredients and add the golden syrup, eggs, oil and milk. Beat well, using a wooden spoon, until smooth and then pour into the prepared tins.

3 Bake for about 35 minutes, until the cakes are well risen and spring back when pressed lightly with the fingertips. Turn out on to a wire rack, remove the lining paper and leave to cool completely. Cut each cake in half horizontally.

4 For the icing, put the chocolate into a bowl placed over a pan of hot water. The water in the pan must not touch the bowl or the chocolate may overheat. Place the pan over a low heat until the chocolate has melted, stirring occasionally, then add the butter and stir until the butter has melted.

5 Put half the cake for the bottom layer on a wire rack and place a baking tray underneath to catch the drips. Spoon a little of the icing on to the cake, spreading it evenly to the sides. Repeat with the remaining cake layers, then pour the remaining icing over the top of the cake and use a small palette knife to smooth it evenly over the top and sides of the cake. Leave to set.

6 For the chocolate waves, melt the white and dark chocolate in separate small bowls over a pan of hot water. Spread the chocolate on to 4 strips of foil about 4 cm (1½ in) wide and 35 cm (14 in) long. Lay the strips carefully over 2 mugs or tins, placed on their sides on a baking tray, to give a wavy shape. Allow to set in the fridge, then carefully peel off the foil and use the chocolate waves to decorate the top of the cake.

Chocolate crispies

This mixture makes 18 small crispies or, for a more generous size, you could do about 12. Keep them cool in warm weather. If you haven't any paper cases, you can spoon the mixture on to baking parchment in mounds and leave to set. When I was small, my mother did them on the wax paper from inside the cornflake packet!

preparation time: 10 minutes
cooking time: none
tins needed: 1 large baking tray
  and 18 paper cake cases
makes 18

225 g (8 oz) plain chocolate,
  broken into pieces
1 tablespoon golden syrup
50 g (2 oz) margarine
75 g (3 oz) cornflakes

1 Put the chocolate into a medium saucepan with the golden syrup and the margarine. Allow to melt over a low heat, stirring occasionally. Meanwhile, put 18 paper cake cases on to a large baking tray.

2 Add the cornflakes to the pan and stir gently until they are all evenly coated in the chocolate mixture.

3 Divide the mixture evenly between the paper cases and place in the refrigerator to set.

Cappuccino cake

Make sure you use the new, deep sandwich tins for this recipe, as the shallower tins tend to overflow. They are available from good cookshops or by mail order from Lakeland Ltd.

preparation time: 20 minutes
cooking time: 25–30 minutes
tins needed: 2 loose-bottomed
20 cm (8 in) sandwich tins,
4 cm (1½ in) deep

50 g (2 oz) cocoa powder

6 tablespoons boiling water

3 eggs

60 ml (2 fl oz) milk

175 g (6 oz) self-raising flour

1 rounded teaspoon baking powder

100 g (4 oz) margarine or butter, softened

275 g (10 oz) caster sugar

For the filling and topping:

300 ml (10 fl oz) double cream

1 teaspoon instant coffee, dissolved in 2 teaspoons hot water

a little cocoa powder or drinking chocolate for dusting

1 Lightly grease the tins and line the bases with non-stick baking parchment. Pre-heat the oven to 180°C/350°F/Gas Mark 4. Put the cocoa powder into a large mixing bowl, add the boiling water and mix well until it has a paste-like consistency.

2 Add all the remaining ingredients to the bowl and whisk with a hand-held electric mixer until just combined. The mixture will be a thickish batter (be careful not to over-whisk).

3 Divide the cake mixture between the prepared tins and gently level the surface. Bake for 25–30 minutes, until the cakes are well risen and beginning to shrink away from the side of the tin. Turn the cakes out on to a wire rack and leave to cool completely.

4 To finish the cake, whip the double cream until it just holds its shape and then stir in the dissolved coffee. Use half the cream to fill the cake and spread the remainder over the top. Gently smooth the surface with a palette knife and dust with sifted cocoa or drinking chocolate. This cake is best eaten fresh; store in the fridge if necessary.

Chocolate and vanilla marble loaf

This loaf cake looks spectacular and is lovely for a special occasion. It easily slices into ten.

preparation time: 30 minutes
cooking time: 1–1½ hours
tin needed: a 900 g (2 lb) loaf tin,
    17 x 9 x 9 cm (6½ x 3½ x 3½ in)
    base measurement

175 g (6 oz) margarine,
    softened

175 g (6 oz) caster sugar

225 g (8 oz) self-raising flour

1½ teaspoons baking powder

3 eggs

1 tablespoon milk

½ teaspoon vanilla extract

1½ tablespoons cocoa powder

2 tablespoons hot water

For the icing:

25 g (1 oz) margarine

15 g (½ oz) cocoa powder,
    sifted

1–2 tablespoons milk

100 g (4 oz) icing sugar, sifted

about 25 g (1 oz) white chocolate, melted

1 Lightly grease the tin and line with a wide strip of non-stick baking parchment to go up the wide sides and over the base of the tin. Pre-heat the oven to 160°C/325°F/Gas Mark 3. Put the margarine, sugar, flour, baking powder, eggs, milk and vanilla extract into a large bowl and beat with a hand-held electric mixer for about 2 minutes, until well blended. Spoon half the mixture into another bowl and set aside.

2 In a small bowl, mix the cocoa powder and hot water together until smooth. Allow to cool slightly, then add to one of the bowls of cake mixture, mixing well until evenly blended.

3 Spoon the vanilla and chocolate cake mixtures randomly into the prepared tin until all of the mixture is used up and gently level the surface. Bake for 50 minutes–1 hour, until the cake is well risen, springy to the touch and beginning to shrink away from the sides of the tin. Allow to cool in the tin for a few minutes, then turn out on to a wire rack, remove the lining paper and leave to cool completely.

4 For the icing, melt the margarine in a small pan, add the cocoa powder, stir to blend and cook gently for 1 minute. Stir in the milk and icing sugar, then remove from the heat and mix thoroughly. If necessary, leave the icing on one side, stirring occasionally, to thicken.

5 Spread the cake evenly with the icing, then drizzle the melted white chocolate over the top. Leave to set.

Chocolate chip cookies

These cookies will keep in a tin for a week. Don't expect them to be as crisp as traditional biscuits – they should be slightly chewy.

For a very adult taste, chop a bar of plain orange chocolate into small cubes and use instead of the chocolate chips.

preparation time: 15 minutes
cooking time: 8–10 minutes
tins needed: 3 baking trays
makes about 20

100 g (4 oz) butter, softened

75 g (3 oz) caster sugar

50 g (2 oz) light muscovado sugar

½ teaspoon vanilla extract

1 large egg, beaten

150 g (5 oz) self-raising flour

100 g (4 oz) plain chocolate chips

1 Lightly grease 3 baking trays. Pre-heat the oven to 190°C/375°F/Gas Mark 5. Measure the butter and sugars into a medium bowl and beat thoroughly with a hand-held electric mixer or wooden spoon until evenly blended.

2 Add the vanilla extract to the beaten egg and then add these gradually to the butter and sugar mixture in the bowl, beating well between each addition. Next, mix in the flour, and lastly stir in the chocolate chips.

3 Spoon large teaspoons of the mixture on to the prepared baking trays, leaving room for the cookies to spread. Bake in the top of the oven for about 8–10 minutes, until the cookies are golden. Watch them like a hawk, as they will turn dark brown very quickly.

4 Allow the cookies to cool on
the trays for a few minutes,
then lift off with a palette
knife or fish slice and place
on a wire cooling rack. Leave
to cool completely, then store
in an airtight tin.

Chocolate éclairs

These are sheer luxury and well worth making. Serve for tea or as a dessert.

preparation time: about 10 minutes, plus filling and icing
cooking time: 30 minutes
tins needed: 2 baking trays
makes about 12

For the choux pastry:
50 g (2 oz) butter, diced
150 ml (5 fl oz) water
65 g (2½ oz) plain flour, sifted
2 eggs, beaten

For the filling:
300 ml (10 fl oz) whipping cream

For the icing:
50 g (2 oz) plain chocolate, broken into pieces
15 g (½ oz) butter
75 g (3 oz) icing sugar, sifted

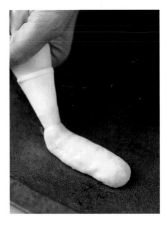

1 Lightly grease 2 baking trays. Pre-heat the oven to 220°C/425°F/Gas Mark 7. To make the choux pastry, put the butter and water into a small pan and place over a low heat. Allow the butter to melt and then bring slowly to the boil. Remove the pan from the heat, add the flour all at once and beat until the mixture forms a soft ball and leaves the side of the pan. Allow to cool slightly.

2 Gradually beat the eggs into the mixture, beating really well between each addition to give a smooth, shiny paste. It is easiest to use a hand-held electric mixer for this, or you can do it by hand if you are prepared to beat the mixture really hard!

3 Spoon the mixture into a large piping bag fitted with a 1 cm (½ in) plain nozzle. Pipe on to the greased baking trays into éclair shapes, about 13–15 cm (5–6 in) long, leaving room for them to spread. Bake for 10 minutes, then reduce the heat to 190°C/375°F/Gas Mark 5 and bake for a further 20 minutes, until well risen and a deep golden brown. (It is important that the éclairs are a good golden brown all over, as any pale, undercooked parts will become soggy once they have cooled.) Remove the éclairs from the oven and split them down one side to allow the steam to escape. Leave to cool on a wire rack.

5 For the icing, put the chocolate into a bowl placed over
a pan of hot water, making
sure the water does not touch
the base of the bowl. Add the
butter and 2 tablespoons of
water to the chocolate and
place the pan over a low
heat until the chocolate has
melted. Remove from the
heat and add the sifted icing
sugar, beating well until
smooth. Spoon the icing over
the top of each éclair, then
leave to set.

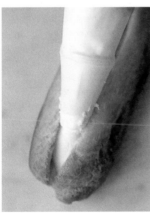

4 Whip the cream until it is just
firm enough to pipe. Fill each
éclair with whipped cream,
using a piping bag fitted with
a plain nozzle.

The ultimate chocolate roulade

Always popular, this roulade freezes very well. Raspberries and chocolate are good together, so add some raspberries (frozen are fine) to the filling if you wish. For a special occasion, scatter masses of fresh raspberries around the roulade on the serving platter – it looks stunning.

preparation time: about 20 minutes, plus several hours' standing
cooking time: 20 minutes
tin needed: a 33 x 23 cm (13 x 9 in) Swiss roll tin

175 g (6 oz) plain chocolate, broken into pieces
175 g (6 oz) caster sugar
6 eggs, separated

2 tablespoons cocoa powder, sifted
300 ml (10 fl oz) double cream
icing sugar

 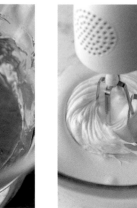 

1 Lightly grease the Swiss roll tin and line with non-stick baking parchment, pushing it into the corners. Pre-heat the oven to 180°C/350°F/Gas Mark 4. Put the chocolate into a bowl placed over a pan of hot water. The water in the pan must not touch the bowl or the chocolate may overheat. Place the pan over a low heat until the chocolate has melted, stirring occasionally. Allow to cool slightly.

2 Put the sugar and egg yolks into a bowl and whisk with a hand-held electric mixer on a high speed until light and creamy. Add the cooled chocolate and stir until evenly blended.

3 Whisk the egg whites in a large mixing bowl until stiff but not dry. Stir a large spoonful of the egg whites into the chocolate mixture, mix gently and then fold in the remaining egg whites, followed by the cocoa powder. Turn the mixture into the prepared tin and gently level the surface. Bake for about 20 minutes, until firm to the touch.

4 Remove the cake from the oven, leave in the tin and place a cooling rack over the top of the cake. Place a clean, damp tea towel on top of the rack and leave for several hours or overnight in a cool place; the cake will sink slightly. (If the tea towel dries out, simply re-dampen it.)

5 Whip the cream until it just holds its shape. Dust a large piece of non-stick baking parchment with icing sugar. Turn the roulade out on to the paper and peel off the lining paper. Spread with the whipped cream and roll up like a Swiss roll, starting with one of the short edges; roll tightly to start with and use the paper to help. Don't worry if it cracks – that is quite normal and part of its charm!

FAVOURITE
CAKES

Victoria sandwich

A great British classic. The all-in-one method makes it very simple to prepare. Vary the jam as you wish. This is one of the few recipes where I have given a choice of butter or margarine. Margarine will give an excellent result, but make sure you use margarine and not a spread with a low fat content.

> preparation time: 15 minutes
> cooking time: 25 minutes
> tins needed: 2 loose-bottomed
> 20 cm (8 in) sandwich tins,
> 4 cm (1½ in) deep

225 g (8 oz) butter or
  margarine, softened
225 g (8 oz) caster sugar
4 eggs
225 g (8 oz) self-raising flour
2 teaspoons baking powder

For the filling and topping:
about 4 tablespoons
  strawberry or raspberry jam
a little caster sugar

1 Lightly grease the tins and line the bases with non-stick baking parchment. Pre-heat the oven to 180°C/350°F/Gas Mark 4. Measure the butter or margarine, sugar, eggs, flour and baking powder into a large bowl and beat for about 2 minutes, until just blended; an electric mixer is best for this, but of course you can also beat by hand with a wooden spoon.

3 Bake for about 25 minutes, until well risen and golden. The tops of the cakes should spring back when pressed lightly with a finger. Leave the cakes to cool in the tins for a few minutes, then run a small palette knife or blunt knife around the edge of the tins to free the sides of the cakes. Turn the cakes out on to a wire rack, peel off the paper and leave to cool completely.

2 Divide the mixture evenly between the prepared tins and level the surface with the back of a spoon or a plastic spatula.

4 Choose the cake with the best top, then put the other cake top downwards on to a serving plate. Spread with the jam, put the other cake on top (top upwards) and sprinkle with caster sugar to serve.

Hokey pokey coffee cake

A special cake from New Zealand. Coffee and walnuts have a natural affinity and make a delicious cake. The addition of walnut praline makes this extra special; save the best pieces to decorate the top of the cake, chop the remainder and add to the icing for the middle.

> preparation time: 20 minutes
> cooking time: 30–35 minutes
> tins needed: 2 loose-bottomed
> 20 cm (8 in) sandwich tins,
> 4 cm (1½ in) deep

225 g (8 oz) margarine, softened

225 g (8 oz) caster sugar

4 eggs

225 g (8 oz) self-raising flour

1 teaspoon baking powder

1½ tablespoons instant coffee, mixed with 1 tablespoon hot water

75 g (3 oz) walnuts, chopped

For the walnut praline:

2 tablespoons water

50 g (2 oz) caster sugar

50 g (2 oz) walnut pieces

For the butter icing:

75 g (3 oz) butter, softened

250 g (9 oz) icing sugar, sifted

1½ teaspoons instant coffee, dissolved in 1½ tablespoons hot water

1 Lightly grease the tins and line the bases with non-stick baking parchment. Pre-heat the oven to 160°C/325°F/Gas Mark 3. Measure all the ingredients for the cake into a mixing bowl and beat until thoroughly blended; an electric mixer is best for this but of course you can also beat by hand with a wooden spoon.

2 Divide the mixture evenly between the prepared tins and gently level the surface with the back of a spoon or a plastic spatula.

3 Bake for 30–35 minutes,
until the cakes are well risen,
golden and beginning to
shrink away from the sides of
the tins. The tops of the cakes
should spring back when
lightly pressed with a finger.
Allow the cakes to cool in the
tins for a few minutes, then
run a small palette knife or
blunt knife around the edge
of the cakes to loosen them.
Turn out on to a wire rack,
peel off the paper and leave
to cool completely.

4 While the cakes are baking,
you can make the praline.
Put the water and caster
sugar into a small pan and
heat gently until the sugar
dissolves. Continue to cook
slowly until the sugar turns
to a nut brown. Watch the
pan like a hawk, as the sugar
can burn quickly.

5 Off the heat, stir in the walnuts, then pour the mixture
out on to non-stick baking
parchment or an oiled baking
tray and leave to cool completely. Roughly break up the
cold, hard praline with your
fingers. Save the best pieces
for the top of the cake, then
chop the remainder to add to
the icing for the middle of
the cake.

6 For the butter icing, put the
butter, icing sugar and dissolved coffee into a small
bowl and mix well until evenly
blended.

7 Select the cake with the best
top, then place the other cake
top downwards on a serving
plate. Spread with half the
butter icing and add the
chopped praline. Place the
second cake on top (top
upwards) and spread with the
remaining butter icing. Use a
small palette knife to spread
the icing neatly, then decorate
with the reserved walnut
praline pieces.

Cherry cake

This classic English cake is perfect to serve with tea. To prevent the cherries sinking to the bottom during cooking, wash the quartered cherries, then dry thoroughly on kitchen paper before adding them to the cake mixture.

preparation time: 15 minutes
cooking time: 1–1½ hours
tin needed: a deep, round 18 cm (7 in) cake tin

150 g (5 oz) glacé cherries
225 g (8 oz) self-raising flour
50 g (2 oz) ground almonds
1½ teaspoons baking powder
200 g (7 oz) butter, softened
200 g (7 oz) caster sugar
4 eggs

1 Lightly grease the cake tin and line the base with a circle of non-stick baking parchment. Pre-heat the oven to 160°C/325°F/Gas Mark 3. Cut each cherry into quarters and rinse under cold running water to remove excess syrup. Drain well and dry very thoroughly on kitchen paper.

2 Place all the remaining ingredients into a large bowl and beat well for about 1 minute to mix thoroughly; an electric mixer is best for this but of course you can also beat by hand with a wooden spoon. Carefully fold in the prepared cherries.

3 Turn the mixture into the prepared tin and bake for 1–1½ hours, until the cake is well risen, golden and firm to the touch. A fine skewer inserted into the centre of the cake should come out clean. Leave the cake to cool in the tin for about 10 minutes, then turn it out on to a wire rack and leave to cool completely.

American apple and apricot cake

This is a new version of a cake that has been a favourite with my family for many years. It can be served with coffee or as a dessert and is best eaten warm.

preparation time: 15 minutes
cooking time: 1¼–1½ hours
tin needed: a deep, round, loose-
  bottomed 20 cm (8 in) cake tin

250 g (9 oz) self-raising flour
1 teaspoon baking powder
225 g (8 oz) caster sugar
2 eggs
½ teaspoon almond extract
150 g (5 oz) butter, melted
225 g (8 oz) cooking apples,
  peeled, cored and thickly
  sliced
100 g (4 oz) ready-to-eat dried
  apricots, snipped into
  pieces
25 g (1 oz) flaked almonds

1 Lightly grease the cake tin and line the base with a circle of non-stick baking parchment. Pre-heat the oven to 160°C/325°F/Gas Mark 3. Put the flour, baking powder, sugar, eggs, almond extract and melted butter into a large bowl. Mix well to combine, then beat well for 1 minute; an electric mixer is best for this but of course you can also beat by hand with a wooden spoon. Add the apples and apricots to the bowl and gently mix them in.

2 Spoon the mixture into the prepared tin, gently level the surface and sprinkle with the flaked almonds.

3 Bake for 1–1½ hours, until the cake is golden, firm to the touch and beginning to shrink away from the side of the tin. Allow to cool in the tin for a few minutes, then turn out on to a plate to serve.

Carrot cake with mascarpone topping

Always a popular cake, this American carrot cake needs to be stored in the fridge because of the mascarpone topping. Walnut pieces are cheaper than walnut halves and are perfect for cakes.

preparation time: 30 minutes
cooking time: 50–60 minutes
tin needed: a deep, round 20 cm (8 in) cake tin

225 g (8 oz) self-raising flour

2 teaspoons baking powder

150 g (5 oz) light muscovado sugar

50 g (2 oz) walnut pieces, chopped

100 g (4 oz) carrots, coarsely grated

2 ripe bananas, mashed

2 eggs

150 ml (5 fl oz) sunflower oil

For the topping:

250 g (9 oz) mascarpone cheese

2–3 teaspoons vanilla extract

2 tablespoons icing sugar, sifted

about 25 g (1 oz) walnut pieces, chopped

1 Lightly grease the cake tin and line the base with a circle of non-stick baking parchment. Pre-heat the oven to 180°C/350°F/Gas Mark 4. Put all the ingredients for the cake into a large bowl and mix until thoroughly blended; an electric mixer is best for this but of course you can also beat by hand with a wooden spoon. Turn the mixture into the prepared cake tin and gently level the surface.

2 Bake for 50–60 minutes, until the cake is well risen, golden and beginning to shrink away from the side of the tin. A fine skewer inserted into the centre of the cake should come out clean. Allow the cake to cool in the tin for a few minutes, then loosen the side of the cake from the tin with a small palette knife or a blunt knife, turn the cake out on to a wire rack and leave to cool completely.

3 For the topping, put the mascarpone cheese into a small bowl, add the vanilla extract, sifted icing sugar and chopped walnuts and beat together. Spread evenly over the top of the cake. Store in the refrigerator.

Lemon drizzle traybake

This really is our top favourite. It is always moist and crunchy. The cake needs to be still warm when the topping is added so that it absorbs the lemon syrup easily, leaving the sugar on top. Do allow the cake to cool a little though – if it is too hot, the syrup will tend to run straight through.

preparation time: 15 minutes
cooking time: 35–40 minutes
tin needed: a traybake or roasting tin, 30 x 23 x 4 cm (12 x 9 x 1½ in)
cuts into 30 squares

225 g (8 oz) butter, softened
225 g (8 oz) caster sugar
275 g (10 oz) self-raising flour
2 teaspoons baking powder
4 eggs
4 tablespoons milk
finely grated zest of 2 lemons

For the crunchy topping:
175 g (6 oz) granulated sugar
juice of 2 lemons

1 Cut a rectangle of non-stick baking parchment to fit the tin. Grease the tin and then line with the paper, pushing it neatly into the corners. Pre-heat the oven to 160°C/325°F/Gas Mark 3. Measure all the ingredients for the traybake into a large bowl and beat well for about 2 minutes, until well blended; an electric mixer is best for this but of course you can also beat by hand with a wooden spoon. Turn the mixture into the prepared tin, scraping the sides of the bowl with a plastic spatula to remove all of the mixture. Level the top gently with the back of the spatula.

2 Bake in the middle of the oven for 35–40 minutes, until the traybake springs back when pressed lightly with a finger in the centre and is beginning to shrink away from the sides of the tin. Allow to cool in the tin for a few minutes, then lift the cake out of the tin still in the lining paper. Carefully remove the paper and put the cake on to a wire rack placed over a tray (to catch drips of the topping).

3 To make the crunchy topping, mix the granulated sugar and lemon juice in a small bowl to give a runny consistency. Spoon this mixture evenly over the traybake while it is still just warm. Cut into 30 squares when cold.

Black cherry Swiss roll

This classic teatime cake is best eaten very fresh, as fatless sponges do not keep for long. Vary the jam as you wish. A table-top electric mixer makes easy work of the whisking but if you don't have one, use a hand-held electric whisk or a balloon whisk and place the bowl containing the eggs and sugar over a pan of hot water.

preparation time: 20 minutes
cooking time: 10 minutes
tin needed: a 33 x 23 cm (13 x 9 in) Swiss roll tin
cuts into 8 generous slices

4 eggs, at room temperature

100 g (4 oz) caster sugar, plus extra for sprinkling

100 g (4 oz) self-raising flour

For the filling:

about 3 tablespoons black cherry jam

300 ml (10 fl oz) double cream, whipped

a few fresh black cherries (optional)

1 Cut a rectangle of non-stick baking parchment just larger than the base and sides of the Swiss roll tin. Grease the tin and then line it with the paper, pushing it neatly into the corners to fit. Pre-heat the oven to 200°C/400°F/Gas Mark 6. Put the eggs and sugar in a large bowl and whisk well, preferably using a table-top or hand-held electric mixer, until the mixture is light and frothy and has increased in volume. When the whisk is lifted, the mixture falling off it should leave a trail on the surface of the mixture in the bowl.

2 Sift the flour into the mixture, carefully folding it in at the same time with a plastic spatula. Turn the mixture into the prepared tin and spread it gently into the corners.

5 Carefully unroll the cooled cake, remove the paper and spread the cake with the jam, followed by the whipped cream. Re-roll the cake, sprinkle with a little more caster sugar if needs be, and, for a special occasion, decorate with a few fresh black cherries. Keep in the fridge until needed but eat as fresh as possible.

3 Bake for 10 minutes or until the sponge begins to shrink away from the sides of the tin and is springy to the touch. Watch the cake very carefully as it is easy to over-bake it.

4 While the cake is cooking, place a piece of non-stick baking parchment a little bigger than the size of the tin on a work surface and sprinkle it with caster sugar. When the cake is done, invert it on to the sugared paper. Quickly loosen the lining paper on the bottom of the cake and

peel it away. Trim the edges of the sponge with a sharp knife and make a score mark 2.5 cm (1 in) in from one shorter edge, being careful not to cut right through. Roll the cake up firmly from the shorter, cut end, with the paper inside, and leave to cool.

Ginger and treacle spiced traybake

Treacle can be difficult to weigh accurately, as it tends to stick to the scale pan. Weighing it on top of the sugar overcomes this problem.

This traybake freezes very well un-iced, and in fact improves with freezing.

preparation time: 20 minutes
cooking time: 35–40 minutes
tin needed: a traybake or roasting tin, 30 x 23 x 4 cm (12 x 9 x 1½ in)
makes 15–20 slices

225 g (8 oz) margarine, softened

175 g (6 oz) light muscovado sugar

200 g (7 oz) black treacle

300 g (11 oz) self-raising flour

2 teaspoons baking powder

1 teaspoon ground mixed spice

1 teaspoon ground allspice

4 eggs

4 tablespoons milk

3 bulbs of stem ginger from a jar, finely chopped

For the icing:

75 g (3 oz) icing sugar

about 3 tablespoons stem ginger syrup from the jar

3 bulbs of stem ginger from a jar, finely chopped

1 Cut a rectangle of non-stick baking parchment to fit the base and sides of the tray-bake or roasting tin. Grease the tin and then line it with the paper, pushing it neatly into the corners. Pre-heat the oven to 180°C/350°F/Gas Mark 4. Put all the ingredients for the traybake into a large bowl and beat for about 2 minutes, until well blended; a hand-held electric mixer is best for this, but of course you can also mix it by hand with a wooden spoon.

2 Turn the mixture into the prepared tin, scraping the bowl with a plastic spatula to remove all the mixture. Level the top gently with the back of the spatula.

3 Bake for 35–40 minutes, until the traybake springs back when pressed lightly with a finger in the centre and is beginning to shrink away from the sides of the tin. Allow to cool a little, then remove the cake from the tin by easing the paper away from the sides of the tin. Turn on to a cooling rack, remove the lining paper and leave to cool completely.

4 To make the icing, sift the icing sugar into a bowl, add the ginger syrup and mix until the icing is smooth and has a spreading consistency. Pour the icing over the cake, spread it gently to the edges with a small palette knife and sprinkle with the chopped stem ginger to decorate. Allow the icing to set before slicing the traybake into 15–20 pieces.

Maple syrup cake

Using maple syrup and pecan nuts, this Canadian-inspired cake is filled and covered with whipped cream, and is a real treat for a special gathering at coffee time. Fill and cover ahead of time, so that the cake keeps moist. Only the orange zest is used, so add the flesh from the oranges to a fruit salad or have fresh orange for breakfast.

preparation time: 25 minutes
cooking time: 1–1½ hours
tin needed: a deep, round, 20 cm (8 in) cake tin

225 g (8 oz) butter, softened
225 g (8 oz) light muscovado sugar
grated zest of 1 orange
4 eggs
100 ml (3½ fl oz) maple syrup

350 g (12 oz) self-raising flour
2 teaspoons baking powder
½ teaspoon ground ginger
50 g (2 oz) pecan nuts, chopped

For the filling and topping:
450 ml (15 fl oz) double cream
2 tablespoons maple syrup
zest of 1 orange, shredded

1 Lightly grease the cake tin and line the base with a circle of non-stick baking parchment. Pre-heat the oven to 160°C/ 325°F/Gas Mark 3. Put all the ingredients for the cake except the pecan nuts into a large bowl and mix well until even-ly blended; an electric mixer is best for this, but of course you can also beat by hand with a wooden spoon. Stir in the chopped pecan nuts.

2 Spoon the mixture into the prepared cake tin and level the surface. Bake for 1–1½ hours, until well risen, golden and springy to the touch. Allow to cool slightly, then turn the cake out on to a wire rack, peel off the lining paper and leave to cool completely.

3 Whip the cream until it just holds its shape and then fold in the maple syrup.

4 Split the cake horizontally into 3 and fill and cover with the cream, using a small palette knife to smooth it evenly over the top and sides. Decorate the top with the shredded orange zest. Store in the refrigerator.

Australian apple and raisin cake

This cake is made with no eggs – useful for those who have an allergy to them. The stewed apple does not have to be a smooth purée – chunks of apple are good in this cake.

preparation time: 25 minutes
cooking time: 50 minutes–1 hour
tin needed: a deep, round, loose-
bottomed 18 cm (7 in) cake tin

1 large cooking apple, peeled, cored and thickly sliced

100 g (4 oz) butter, softened

100 g (4 oz) light muscovado sugar

1 teaspoon bicarbonate of soda

175 g (6 oz) self-raising flour

1 teaspoon cocoa powder

½ teaspoon freshly grated nutmeg

½ teaspoon ground cinnamon

75 g (3 oz) raisins

a little icing sugar for dusting

1 Lightly grease the tin and line the base with a circle of non-stick baking parchment. Pre-heat the oven to 160°C/325°F/Gas Mark 3. Put the apple slices into a small pan, add a very little water and cook gently until tender. Stir the apple mixture to break it down a little, but it doesn't need to be a smooth purée. Remove from the heat and leave until just warm.

2 Put the butter and sugar into a large bowl and beat together until evenly blended; an electric mixer is best for this but of course you can also beat by hand with a wooden spoon. Mix together the warm apple and the bicarbonate of soda in a small bowl (the mixture will froth up, but don't worry: this is quite normal). Add to the butter and sugar and stir to mix.

3 Sift the flour, cocoa powder, nutmeg and cinnamon into the mixture, add the raisins and fold in gently, using a plastic spatula or a large metal spoon. Turn into the prepared cake tin and gently level the surface with a spatula or the back of a spoon.

4 Bake in the middle of the oven for 50 minutes–1 hour, until the cake is golden brown in colour, springy to the touch and has begun to shrink away from the side of the tin. Allow to cool in the tin for 5–10 minutes, then turn out, remove the base paper and leave on a wire rack to cool completely. Dust lightly with icing sugar before serving.

Family fruit teabread

You need to start this teabread the day before, as the dried fruits have to be soaked in hot tea overnight to give them time to swell. If you have tea left in the pot, use that instead of making it specially. Teabreads packed with fruit such as this one are known as bara brith in Wales, barm brack in Ireland and Selkirk bannock in Scotland. They are all good served buttered, and they keep well. Allow to cool completely, then store in an airtight tin or polythene bag.

preparation time: 15 minutes,
  plus soaking overnight
cooking time: 1¼–1½ hours
tin needed: a 900 g (2 lb) loaf tin,
  17 x 9 x 9 cm (6½ x 3½ x 3½ in)
  base measurement

350 g (12 oz) mixed dried fruit
225 g (8 oz) light muscovado
  sugar
300 ml (10 fl oz) hot Earl Grey
  tea, made using 2 teaspoons
  Earl Grey tea or 2 tea bags
275 g (10 oz) self-raising flour
finely grated zest of 1 lemon
1 egg, beaten

1 Put the mixed dried fruit and the sugar into a medium bowl, stir to mix, then pour over the hot tea. Cover the bowl and leave in a cool place overnight to allow the fruit to plump up.

2 The next day, lightly grease the tin and line it with a wide strip of non-stick baking parchment to go up the wide sides and over the base. Pre-heat the oven to 150°C/300°F/Gas Mark 2. Add the flour, lemon zest and beaten egg to the fruit mixture and stir with a wooden spoon until thoroughly mixed.

3 Turn the mixture into the pre-pared tin and gently level the surface. Bake in the middle of the oven for 1¼–1½ hours, until the teabread is well risen and firm to the touch and a fine skewer inserted in the centre comes out clean. Leave to cool in the tin for about 10 minutes, then loosen with a small palette knife. Turn the teabread out and leave on a wire rack to cool. Remove the lining paper and serve sliced and buttered.

Banana loaf

This is a lovely, moist loaf, which really doesn't need to be buttered. It freezes extremely well. Any bananas left in the fruit bowl are ideal for this cake – the riper they are, the better.

preparation time: 15 minutes
cooking time: 1 hour
tin needed: a 900 g (2 lb) loaf tin, 17 x 9 x 9 cm (6½ x 3½ x 3½ in) base measurement

100 g (4 oz) butter, softened
175 g (6 oz) caster sugar
2 eggs
2 ripe bananas, mashed
225 g (8 oz) self-raising flour
1 teaspoon baking powder
2 tablespoons milk

1 Lightly grease the loaf tin and line it with non-stick baking parchment. Pre-heat the oven to 180°C/350°F/Gas Mark 4. Measure all the ingredients into a mixing bowl and beat for about 2 minutes, until well blended; an electric mixer is best for this but of course you can also beat by hand with a wooden spoon.

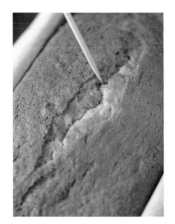

2 Spoon the mixture into the prepared tin and level the surface. Bake for about 1 hour, until well risen and golden brown. A fine skewer inserted in the centre of the cake should come out clean.

3 Leave the cake to cool in the tin for a few minutes, then loosen with a small palette knife and turn the cake out. Remove the lining paper and leave on a wire rack to cool completely. Slice thickly to serve.

Classic sticky gingerbread

This keeps and freezes extremely well. Sometimes you get a dip in the middle of the gingerbread, which indicates that you have been a bit heavy-handed with the syrup and treacle. It just means it tastes even more moreish.

preparation time: 15 minutes

cooking time: 50 minutes

tin needed: a traybake or roasting tin, 30 x 23 x 4 cm (12 x 9 x 1½ in)

cuts into 16 generous pieces

225 g (8 oz) margarine or butter

225 g (8 oz) light muscovado sugar

225 g (8 oz) golden syrup

225 g (8 oz) black treacle

225 g (8 oz) self-raising flour

225 g (8 oz) wholemeal self-raising flour

4 teaspoons ground ginger

2 eggs

300 ml (10 fl oz) milk

1 Cut a rectangle of non-stick baking parchment to fit the base and sides of the tin. Lightly grease the tin and then line it with the paper, pushing it neatly into the corners. Pre-heat the oven to 160°C/325°F/Gas Mark 3. Measure the margarine or butter, sugar, golden syrup and black treacle into a medium pan and heat gently until the mixture has melted evenly. Allow to cool slightly.

3 Pour the mixture into the pre-pared tin, tilt gently to level the surface and bake for about 50 minutes, until well risen, golden and springy to the touch. Allow the ginger-bread to cool a little in the tin, then turn out on to a wire rack and leave to cool completely. Cut into 16 squares.

2 Put the flours and ground ginger into a large mixing bowl and stir together lightly. Beat the eggs into the milk. Pour the cooled margarine and syrup mixture into the flour with the egg and milk mixture and beat with a wooden spoon until smooth.

Celebration cake

I use this for Christmas, birthdays and all special occasions – it's a winner. Start preparing the cake the night before you want to bake it, as the dried fruits need to be soaked in brandy so that they become plump. You can vary the fruit if you like but make the total weight the same as in the recipe.

preparation time: about 30 minutes, plus overnight soaking
cooking time: 4–4½ hours
tin needed: a deep, round 23 cm (9 in) cake tin

350 g (12 oz) currants

225 g (8 oz) sultanas

225 g (8 oz) raisins

175 g (6 oz) glacé cherries, quartered, rinsed and dried

175 g (6 oz) ready-to-eat dried apricots, snipped into pieces

75 g (3 oz) mixed candied peel, finely chopped

4 tablespoons brandy, plus extra to 'feed' the cake

275 g (10 oz) plain flour

scant ½ teaspoon grated nutmeg

½ teaspoon ground mixed spice

400 g (14 oz) butter, softened

400 g (14 oz) dark muscovado sugar

5 eggs

65 g (2½ oz) whole almonds, chopped (no need to remove the skins)

1 tablespoon black treacle

grated zest of 1 lemon

grated zest of 1 orange

To decorate:

whole blanched almonds

glacé cherries, halved, rinsed and dried

1 Put the currants, sultanas, raisins, cherries, apricots and chopped mixed peel into a large bowl. Stir in the brandy, cover the bowl and leave in a cool place overnight.

2 The next day, lightly grease the cake tin. Cut a strip of non-stick baking parchment to fit twice around the sides of the tin. Fold the bottom edge of the strip up by about 2.5 cm (1 in), creasing it firmly, then open out the fold and cut slanting lines into this narrow strip at intervals. Put a circle of non-stick baking parchment into the base of the tin, lightly grease the outer edge and then fit the prepared strip of parchment with the snipped edge in the base of the tin to line the sides. Place a second circle of non-stick baking parchment in the tin to cover the cut part of the paper.

3 Pre-heat the oven to 140°C/ 275°F/Gas Mark 1. Measure the flour, grated nutmeg, mixed spice, butter, sugar, eggs, chopped almonds, black treacle and grated lemon and orange zest into a large bowl and beat well to mix thoroughly; an electric mixer is best for this but of course you can also beat by hand with a wooden spoon. Fold in the soaked fruits.

4 Spoon the mixture into the prepared cake tin and spread out evenly with the back of the spoon. Decorate the top with blanched almonds and halved glacé cherries, pushing them lightly into the top of the cake mixture. Cover the top of the cake loosely with a double layer of grease-proof paper and bake for 4–4½ hours, until the cake feels firm to the touch and a skewer inserted into the centre comes out clean. Allow the cake to cool in the tin.

5 When the cake is almost cold, remove it from the tin and peel off the lining paper. Pierce the base at intervals with a fine skewer and feed with a little brandy. Once the cake is completely cold, wrap it in a double layer of grease-proof paper and then in foil. Store in a cool place for up to 3 months, feeding at intervals with more brandy.

BITE-SIZED
CAKES

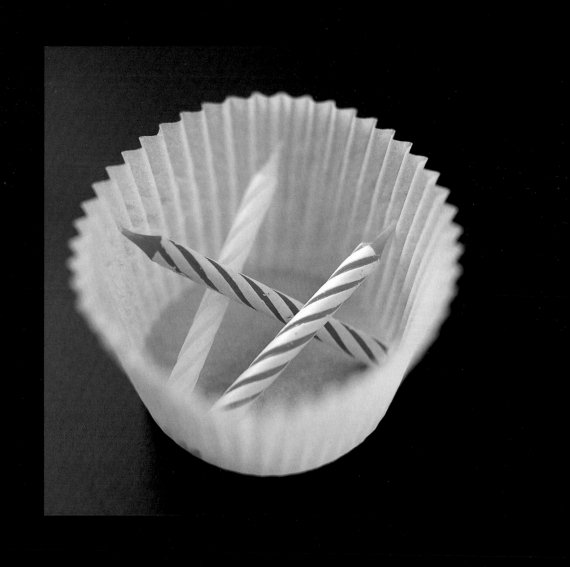

Orange Scotch pancakes

In the old days, these were made on a solid metal griddle over an open fire. Now it is more practical to use a large, non-stick frying pan. Serve as soon as they are made, with butter and syrup. If you do make them in advance and need to reheat them, arrange in a single layer on an ovenproof plate, cover tightly with foil and reheat in a moderate oven for about 10 minutes.

preparation time: 10 minutes
cooking time: about 2–3 minutes
 per batch
makes about 24

2 oranges

a little milk

175 g (6 oz) self-raising flour

1 teaspoon baking powder

40 g (1½ oz) caster sugar

1 egg

a little oil or white vegetable
    fat for greasing

butter and golden syrup or
    maple syrup to serve

1 Grate the zest from the oranges and set aside, and then squeeze the juice. Pour the juice into a measuring jug and make it up to 200 ml (7 fl oz) with milk.

2 Put the flour, baking powder, sugar and orange zest into a mixing bowl. Make a well in the centre and add the egg and half of the orange juice and milk mixture. Beat well to make a smooth, thick batter and then beat in enough of the remaining orange juice and milk to give a batter the consistency of thick cream.

3 Heat a large, non-stick frying pan over a medium heat and grease with a little oil or white vegetable fat. Drop the mixture in dessertspoonfuls on to the hot pan, spacing them well apart to allow the mixture to spread.

4 When bubbles appear on the surface, turn the pancakes over with a blunt-ended non-stick palette knife or a spatula and cook on the other side for 30 seconds–1 minute, until golden brown. Transfer to a wire rack and cover with a clean tea towel to keep them soft. Cook the remaining mixture in the same way. Serve at once, with butter and golden or maple syrup, and orange zest, if liked.

Devonshire scones

The secret of good scones is not to handle them too much before baking, and to make the mixture on the wet, sticky side. Either eat the scones on the day of making or leave them to cool completely and then freeze. If time allows, thaw them at room temperature for a couple of hours and then refresh in a moderate oven for about 10 minutes. If you like large scones, this amount of mixture will make eight to ten 9 cm (3½ in) scones.

preparation time: 15 minutes
cooking time: 10–15 minutes
tins needed: 2 baking trays
makes about 20

450 g (1 lb) self-raising flour
2 rounded teaspoons baking powder
75 g (3 oz) butter, at room temperature
50 g (2 oz) caster sugar
2 eggs
about 225 ml (8 fl oz) milk

1 Lightly grease 2 baking trays. Pre-heat the oven to 220°C/ 425°F/Gas Mark 7. Put the flour and baking powder into a large bowl. Add the butter and rub it in with your fingertips until the mixture resembles fine breadcrumbs. Stir in the sugar.

2 Beat the eggs together and make up to a generous 300 ml (10 fl oz) with the milk, then put about 2 tablespoons of the mixture aside in a cup for glazing the scones later. Gradually add the egg mixture to the dry ingredients, stirring it in until you have a soft dough. It is far better that the scone mixture is on the wet side, sticking to your fingers, as the scones will rise better.

3 Turn the dough on to a lightly floured surface and flatten it out with your hand or a rolling pin to a thickness of 1–2 cm (½–1 in).

5 Arrange the scones on the greased baking trays and brush the tops with the reserved beaten egg mixture to glaze. Bake for 10–15 minutes, until well risen and golden, then transfer to a wire rack and leave to cool, covered with a clean tea towel to keep them moist. Serve as fresh as possible, cut in half and spread generously with strawberry jam. Top with a good spoon-ful of thick cream as well, if you like.

4 Use a 5 cm (2 in) fluted cutter to stamp out the scones by pushing the cutter straight down into the dough (as opposed to twisting it), then lifting it straight out. This ensures that the scones will rise evenly and keep their shape. Gently push the remaining dough together, knead very lightly then re-roll and cut out more scones.

Blueberry muffins

Best served warm, these are wonderful for breakfast. Don't expect them to be sweet like a cake – they are more like scones.

Paper muffin cases are available from good supermarkets. They are not essential but they do make life easier when extracting the muffins from the tins!

preparation time: 15 minutes
cooking time: 20–25 minutes
tin needed: a deep, 12-hole
  muffin tin
makes 12

275 g (10 oz) plain flour
1 tablespoon baking powder
75 g (3 oz) caster sugar
grated zest of 1 lemon
2 eggs
225 ml (8 fl oz) milk
100 g (4 oz) butter, melted
½ teaspoon vanilla extract
225 g (8 oz) blueberries

1 Thoroughly grease the muffin tins or put a paper muffin case into each muffin 'hole' or on a baking tray. Pre-heat the oven to 200°C/400°F/Gas Mark 6. Measure the flour, baking powder, sugar and grated lemon zest into a mixing bowl and stir briefly to combine. Mix together the eggs, milk, cooled melted butter and vanilla extract and then add these to the dry ingredients.

2 Mix quickly but gently to blend the ingredients together. Don't overmix; it doesn't need to be a smooth mixture, as long as the dry ingredients are incorporated. Gently stir in the blueberries.

3 Spoon the mixture into the muffin tin, filling it almost to the top. Bake for 20–25 minutes, until well risen, golden and firm to the touch. Allow to cool for a few minutes in the tin, then lift out and cool for a little longer on a wire rack. Serve warm. If you have made the muffins ahead and want to reheat them, pop them in a low oven for a few minutes.

Mini St Clements muffins

These are not breakfast muffins and are therefore sweeter. They are delicious at any time and children love them, too. It is easier to use small paper cases to line the mini-muffin tins. If you don't have any cases, grease the tins well and leave the muffins to cool before trying to remove them – if you try to remove them when they are hot, they tend to come apart!

preparation time: about 10 minutes
cooking time: 15 minutes
tins needed: 2 x 12-hole mini-
  muffin tins
makes about 24

1 thin-skinned orange,
  washed
grated zest of 1 lemon
100 g (4 oz) caster sugar
1 egg
100 ml (3½ fl oz) milk

50 g (2 oz) butter, melted and
  cooled slightly
1 teaspoon baking powder
175 g (6 oz) self-raising flour
icing sugar for dusting

3 Spoon the mixture into the lined mini-muffin tins, filling them almost to the top. Bake for about 15 minutes, until well risen, golden and firm to the touch. Lift the paper cases out of the tin. Dust with icing sugar and serve while still warm.

1 Line the mini-muffin tins with paper cases. Pre-heat the oven to 200°C/400°F/Gas Mark 6. Cut the whole orange into chunks and remove any pips with the point of a knife. Process the orange in a food processor until finely chopped.

2 Put all the remaining ingredi-ents except the icing sugar into a mixing bowl and beat quickly with a wooden spoon until just mixed. Gently stir in the chopped orange.

Flapjacks

Always extremely popular and very fast to make, flapjacks keep well in an airtight container. You will get different results depending on which type of oats you use — whole oats or jumbo oats don't absorb as much of the melted mixture as rolled oats do, so the flapjacks will be more syrupy but equally delicious! To weigh the syrup, first weigh the sugar, then spread the sugar over the scale pan and measure the syrup on top to make a total weight of 300 g (11 oz). This mixture can also be baked in a traybake or roasting tin, 30 x 23 x 4 cm (12 x 9 x 1½ in).

preparation time: 10 minutes
cooking time: 30 minutes
tins needed: 2 x 20 cm (8 in)
  sandwich tins
makes 16

225 g (8 oz) margarine
225 g (8 oz) demerara sugar
75 g (3 oz) golden syrup
275 g (10 oz) rolled oats

1 Grease the tins and line the bases with non-stick baking parchment. Pre-heat the oven to 160°C/325°F/Gas Mark 3. Put the margarine, sugar and syrup into a medium saucepan and heat gently until the margarine has melted and the sugar dissolved. Remove the pan from the heat and stir in the rolled oats.

2 Turn the mixture into the prepared tins and press down firmly with the back of a spoon to level the surface. Bake for about 30 minutes, until golden brown. Take care not to overbake the flapjacks or they will be very hard.

3 Loosen the edges of the flapjacks from the sides of the tins with a small, flexible palette knife, then leave to cool in the tins for about 10 minutes. Tip the flapjacks out on to a plate and slice each round into 8 wedges. Leave on a wire rack to cool completely.

Lavender biscuits

Both the leaves and the flowers of lavender can be used, although it is best to use young leaves. Dried lavender is stronger in flavour, so use about half the quantity.

preparation time: 15 minutes, plus chilling
cooking time: 15–20 minutes
tins needed: 3 large baking trays
makes about 40

175 g (6 oz) unsalted butter, softened

2 tablespoons fresh lavender flowers and leaves, finely chopped (pick the little flowerlets and the leaves off the stems to measure), or 1 tablespoon dried lavender

100 g (4 oz) caster sugar

225 g (8 oz) plain flour

about 25 g (1 oz) demerara sugar

2 Beat the caster sugar into the butter and lavender and then stir in the flour, bringing the mixture together with your hands and kneading lightly until smooth.

3 Divide the mixture in half and roll out to form two sausage shapes 15 cm (6 in) long. Roll the biscuit 'sausages' in the demerara sugar until evenly coated. Wrap in non-stick baking parchment or foil and chill until firm. Pre-heat the oven to 160°C/325°F/Gas Mark 3.

1 Lightly grease 3 large baking trays. Put the softened butter and the lavender into a mixing bowl and beat together (this will obtain the maximum flavour from the lavender).

4 Cut each 'sausage' into about 20 slices and put them on the prepared baking trays, allowing a little room for them to spread. Bake for 15–20 minutes, until the biscuits are pale golden brown at the edges. Lift them off the trays with a fish slice or palette knife and leave on a wire rack to cool completely.

Diggers

Sometimes known as Anzac biscuits, these hail from Australia. They are very popular with children and are also great served with ice cream or a mousse for dessert.

preparation time: 15 minutes
cooking time: 8–10 minutes
tins needed: 3 baking trays
makes about 45

150 g (5 oz) butter

1 rounded tablespoon golden syrup

175 g (6 oz) granulated sugar

75 g (3 oz) self-raising flour

75 g (3 oz) desiccated coconut

100 g (4 oz) porridge oats

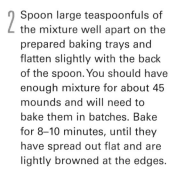

1 Lightly grease 3 baking trays. Pre-heat the oven to 180°C/ 350°F/Gas Mark 4. Measure the butter, golden syrup and sugar into a medium saucepan and heat gently until melted. Stir in the flour, coconut and oats and mix well until evenly blended.

2 Spoon large teaspoonfuls of the mixture well apart on the prepared baking trays and flatten slightly with the back of the spoon. You should have enough mixture for about 45 mounds and will need to bake them in batches. Bake for 8–10 minutes, until they have spread out flat and are lightly browned at the edges.

3 Leave to cool on the trays for a few moments, then carefully lift off with a palette knife and place on a wire rack to cool completely. If the biscuits harden too much to lift off the tray, pop them back into the oven for a few minutes to soften. Store in an airtight tin.

Butter shortbread

This is the traditional butter shortbread but it is also very good with a flavouring of orange. Just add the finely grated zest of one large orange to the mixture. I like to use semolina to give the shortbread crunch, but if you haven't got any you can use cornflour instead.

preparation time: 15 minutes
cooking time: 30–40 minutes
tin needed: a traybake or roasting
 tin, 30 x 23 x 4 cm (12 x 9 x 11½ in)
cuts into about 30 fingers

225 g (8 oz) plain flour

100 g (4 oz) caster sugar

225 g (8 oz) butter, at room
 temperature

100 g (4 oz) semolina

25 g (1 oz) demerara sugar

1 Lightly grease the tin and cut a rectangle of foil to fit the base so that you don't risk marking the tin when cutting the shortbread. Lightly grease the foil. Pre-heat the oven to 160°C/325°F/Gas Mark 3. Put the flour, caster sugar, butter and semolina into a food processor and process until the mixture is thoroughly combined and comes together to form a dough. (This can also be done by hand, rubbing the butter into the flour first, then adding the sugar and semolina and working the ingredients together to form a ball.)

2 Press the dough into the prepared tin and level it with the back of a spatula or a palette knife to ensure that the mixture is an even thickness. Sprinkle the top with the demerara sugar.

3 Bake for 30–40 minutes, until the shortbread is pale golden and cooked through. Keep an eye on it in case it gets too brown. Allow the shortbread to cool in the tin for a few minutes, then cut it into about 30 fingers (10 x 3). Carefully lift the shortbread fingers out of the tin with a small palette knife and place on a wire rack to cool completely. Store in an airtight tin.

MERINGUES, TARTS AND PASTRIES

Meringues

Meringues should be creamy in colour, not ice white, or they look as though they were bought from a shop. They store well in an airtight tin or plastic container – layer them with kitchen paper to protect them from breaking.

preparation time: 15 minutes

cooking time: 1–1½ hours

tins needed: 2 baking trays

makes about 9

3 egg whites

175 g (6 oz) caster sugar

300 ml (10 fl oz) whipping cream, whipped

icing sugar for dusting (optional)

1 Line 2 baking trays with non-stick baking parchment. Preheat the oven to 120°C/250°F/Gas Mark ½. Put the egg whites in a large mixing bowl and whisk on high speed with an electric whisk until stiff but not dry.

2 Add the caster sugar, one teaspoonful at a time, whisking well after each addition, still on high speed, until all the sugar has been added. The meringue should be stiff and glossy.

3 Fit a 1 cm (½ in) plain nozzle into a large nylon piping bag and stand, nozzle down, in a large measuring jug. Fold down the top of the piping bag and spoon the meringue into the bag. Squeeze the meringue mixture towards the nozzle and twist the top of the piping bag to seal. Pipe the meringue into about 18 shells on the prepared baking trays – squeeze the piping bag so that you get a base of

meringue about 5 cm (2 in) in diameter, then lift the bag slightly to form a smaller circle and then finally a smaller circle on top. This is easier to do than it sounds!

Alternatively, use 2 dessertspoons to shape the mixture into oval shells.

4 Bake the meringues for about 1–1½ hours, until they are a creamy colour and can be lifted easily from the paper without sticking. Turn off the oven, leave the door ajar and leave the meringues in the oven until cold.

5 To serve, sandwich the meringues together in pairs with the whipped cream and pile them up on a serving plate. Dust with icing sugar, if liked.

Pavlova

Don't worry if the Pavlova cracks on the top – this is all part of its charm.

preparation time: 15 minutes
cooking time: 1–1½ hours
tin needed: 1 large baking tray

4 egg whites

225 g (8 oz) caster sugar

2 teaspoons cornflour

2 teaspoons white wine vinegar

300 ml (10 fl oz) whipping cream, whipped

about 350 g (12 oz) mixed strawberries, raspberries and kiwi fruit

1 Lay a sheet of non-stick baking parchment on a baking tray and mark a 23 cm (9 in) circle on it. Pre-heat the oven to 160°C/325°F/Gas Mark 3. Put the egg whites in a large bowl and whisk on high speed with an electric whisk until they are stiff and cloud-like. Add the sugar, one tea-spoonful at a time, still whisk-ing at full speed, until it has all been used and the meringue is stiff and glossy. Blend the cornflour and white wine vinegar together in a small bowl and whisk into the meringue mixture.

2 Spoon the mixture into the circle marked on the parch-ment on the baking tray and spread it out gently so that the meringue forms a 23 cm (9 in) circle, building the sides up well so that they are higher than the middle.

3 Place in the pre-heated oven but immediately reduce the temperature to 150°C/300°F/ Gas Mark 2. Bake the Pavlova for 1–1½ hours, until firm to the touch and pale beige in colour. Turn off the oven, leave the door ajar and leave the Pavlova in it until cold.

4 Carefully remove the Pavlova from the baking parchment, slide it on to a flat serving plate and top with the whipped cream. Halve any large strawberries and peel and slice the kiwi fruit. Arrange the fruit on top of the cream. Leave the Pavlova in the fridge for about 1 hour before serving.

Lemon meringue roulade

This meringue needs to be made with white caster sugar as opposed to golden caster sugar, which can give the baked meringue an unappetising grey colour. The roulade freezes well when completed and filled.

preparation time: 15 minutes
cooking time: about 25 minutes
tin needed: a 33 x 23 cm (13 x 9 in) Swiss roll tin
cuts into 8 slices

5 egg whites

275 g (10 oz) white caster sugar

50 g (2 oz) flaked almonds

300 ml (10 fl oz) double cream

grated zest of 1 lemon

2 generous tablespoons good lemon curd

icing sugar for dusting

8 cape gooseberries (physalis), the casing turned back

1 Line the Swiss roll tin with greased non-stick baking parchment. Pre-heat the oven to 200°C/400°F/Gas Mark 6. Put the egg whites in a large bowl and whisk on high speed with an electric whisk until very stiff.

2 Add the sugar one teaspoonful at a time, whisking well between each addition and still on high speed, until all the sugar has been added and the mixture is very, very stiff.

3 Spoon the meringue into the prepared tin and level the surface. Sprinkle with the flaked almonds. Place the tin fairly near the top of the pre-heated oven and bake for about 10 minutes, until pale golden. Lower the oven temperature to 160°C/325°F/Gas Mark 3 and bake for a further 15 minutes, until firm to the touch.

4 Remove the baked meringue from the oven and turn almond-side down on to a sheet of non-stick baking parchment. Remove the paper from the base of the cooked meringue and allow to cool for about 10 minutes.

5 Meanwhile, whisk the cream until it stands in peaks and fold in the grated lemon zest and lemon curd.

6 Spread the cream over the cooled meringue and then, starting from the long end, roll the meringue up fairly tightly to form a roulade. Wrap in non-stick baking parchment and chill before serving. Transfer to a serving plate, dust with icing sugar and arrange the cape gooseberries on top.

Pecan pie

Maple syrup is now available in most good supermarkets but if you cannot find any, substitute 150 g (5 oz) golden syrup mixed with 1 tablespoon black treacle and made up to 200 ml (7 fl oz) with boiling water.

> preparation time: 35 minutes, plus 30 minutes' chilling
> cooking time: 50–55 minutes
> tin needed: a loose-bottomed 23 cm (9 in) fluted flan tin

25 g (1 oz) butter, softened
175 g (6 oz) light muscovado sugar
3 eggs
200 ml (7 fl oz) maple syrup
1 teaspoon vanilla extract
75 g (3 oz) pecan halves

For the rich shortcrust pastry:
175 g (6 oz) plain flour
15 g (½ oz) icing sugar
75 g (3 oz) butter, diced
1 egg yolk
about 1 tablespoon cold water

3 Roll out the pastry on a lightly floured work surface and use to line the flan tin. Prick the pastry all over with a fork, line with non-stick baking parchment or foil, fill with baking beans and bake blind for about 15 minutes. Remove the baking beans and paper and return the pastry case to the oven for 5 minutes or until it is pale golden and dried out. Reduce the oven temperature to 180°C/350°F/Gas Mark 4.

1 Pre-heat the oven to 200°C/400°F/Gas Mark 6. To make the pastry, place the flour and icing sugar in a large bowl and rub in the butter with your fingertips until the mixture resembles fine breadcrumbs.

2 Add the egg yolk and water and mix until it comes together to form a firm dough. (This can, of course, be done in a food processor.) Wrap in cling film and leave to rest in the fridge for about 30 minutes.

4 For the filling, beat the soft-ened butter with the light muscovado sugar. Add the eggs, maple syrup and vanilla extract and beat well.

5 Put the flan tin on a baking tray, arrange the pecan nuts over the pastry, flat side down, then pour in the filling. Bake at the reduced tempera-ture of 180°C/350°F/Gas Mark 4 for 30–35 minutes, until set. The filling will rise up in the oven but will fall back on cooling. Leave to cool, then serve warm, with cream or ice-cream.

Key lime pie

Key lime pie is a speciality of Florida, where limes grow on the low coral islands – the Keys. There are many adaptations of the original. This is mine – a very quick and delicious uncooked version. Make sure you use a loose-bottomed tin.

preparation time: 30 minutes
cooking time: none
tin needed: a loose-bottomed
   20 cm (8 in) sandwich tin

4 large limes
400 g (14 oz) can of condensed
   milk
450 ml (15 fl oz) double cream

For the base:
150 g (5 oz) digestive biscuits
65 g (2½ oz) butter
25 g (1 oz) demerara sugar

1 For the base, put the digestive biscuits into a polythene bag and crush them to crumbs with a rolling pin. Melt the butter in a small pan, remove from the heat and stir in the crushed biscuits and the demerara sugar. Mix well, then spread the mixture over the base and sides of the sandwich tin, pressing it with the back of a metal spoon to make it firm.

2 Remove the rind from 1 of the limes with a zester and set aside to decorate the top of the pie. Squeeze the juice from all the limes.

3 Put the lime juice, condensed milk and 300 ml (10 fl oz) of the double cream into a mixing bowl and whisk until well blended. Pour into the prepared crumb crust and gently level the surface. Chill for several hours, until set, then push up the tin from the base to remove the ring.

4 To decorate, whip the remaining double cream until it just holds its shape, then either spread over the surface of the pie or spoon it in blobs around the edge. Decorate with the reserved lime zest. Serve well chilled.

Banoffi pie

The combination of toffee, bananas and cream makes this one of the most popular desserts around. Make sure you use a non-stick pan for the toffee and watch it very closely, as it can burn easily. Most condensed milk cans now have ring pulls, so the old method of simmering the can in a pan of water for 4 hours to caramelize the condensed milk is not advised.

preparation time: 20 minutes
cooking time: 5 minutes
tin needed: a loose-bottomed
  23 cm (9 in) fluted flan tin

100 g (4 oz) butter
100 g (4 oz) light muscovado
  sugar
2 x 400 g (14 oz) cans of
  condensed milk

For the base:
175 g (6 oz) ginger biscuits
65 g (2½ oz) butter

For the topping:
300 ml (10 fl oz) double cream
1 large banana
a little lemon juice
a little grated milk chocolate
  or plain chocolate

1 For the base, put the ginger biscuits into a polythene bag and crush them to crumbs with a rolling pin. Melt the butter in a small pan, remove from the heat and stir in the crushed biscuits. Mix well, then spread the mixture over the base and sides of the flan tin, pressing it with the back of a metal spoon to make it firm.

2 Put the butter and light muscovado sugar in a roomy non-stick pan. Heat gently until the butter has melted and the sugar has dissolved, then add the condensed milk. Stir continuously and evenly with a flat-ended wooden spatula for about 5 minutes or until the mixture is thick and has turned a golden toffee colour – take care, as it burns easily. Turn it into the prepared crumb crust and leave to cool and set.

3 For the topping, whip the double cream until it just holds its shape and spread it evenly over the cold toffee mixture. Peel and slice the banana and coat it in a little lemon juice to prevent it discolouring. Pile the banana slices on to the middle of the cream and dust the whole pie with grated chocolate. Remove the ring and transfer to a flat plate. Serve well chilled.

Spiced apple strudel

Filo pastry comes in various sizes. If the one you buy is a different size, just adapt step 2, below, so that you have the same finished size.

This strudel is best eaten warm – the pastry will go soggy if left too long.

preparation time: 30 minutes
cooking time: 35–40 minutes
tin needed: 1 large baking tray
cuts into 6–8 slices

about 6 sheets of filo pastry

50 g (2 oz) butter, melted

25 g (1 oz) fresh white bread-crumbs

For the filling:

1 large cooking apple (about 350 g/12 oz peeled weight), peeled, cored and roughly sliced

finely grated zest and juice of ½ lemon

50 g (2 oz) demerara sugar

1 teaspoon ground cinnamon

For the icing:

Juice of ½ lemon

about 100 g (4 oz) icing sugar, sifted

1 Lightly grease a large baking tray. Pre-heat the oven to 190°C/375°F/Gas Mark 5. Mix all the filling ingredients together in a bowl and set aside.

2 Place 2 sheets of filo, long sides together, side by side on a board or work surface, slightly overlapping them. Altogether they should measure about 36 x 30 cm (14 x 12 in). Brush with a little of the melted butter.

3 Top with another layer of filo, overlapping the long sides of the filo sheets again and placing them across the first two sheets. Brush with melted butter and then add the final two layers of filo, overlapping them vertically, like the first layer. Sprinkle the top sheets with the breadcrumbs.

4 Spoon the apple filling over one of the top sheets of pastry, about 5 cm (2 in) in from the long edge and the sides. Cut away about 2.5 cm (1 in) of pastry at the sides of the uncovered sheets of filo – this helps to prevent too much pastry being folded together.

5 Fold the sides in and roll the pastry up from the filling end into a sausage shape. Carefully lift the strudel on to the greased baking tray and brush it all over with melted butter. Bake for about 35–40 minutes, until the pastry is golden and crisp.

6 For the icing, mix the lemon juice with the icing sugar to make a thin icing. (Take care that it is not too thin, though, or it will slide straight off the strudel.) Drizzle the icing over the strudel. Trim the ends off at a diagonal angle (enjoy these as cook's perks!), cut into slices and serve with crème fraîche or just cream.

Blueberry and summer fruit cheesecake

Expect the cheesecake to dip in the centre when it is cooked. That's how it should be, giving a generous space to fill with the fruit.

preparation time: 30 minutes
cooking time: 1–1½ hours
tin needed: a loose-bottomed, round 23 cm (9 in) cake tin

50 g (2 oz) butter, softened

175 g (6 oz) caster sugar

450 g (1 lb) curd cheese (medium-fat soft cheese)

25 g (1 oz) plain flour

finely grated zest and juice of 1 lemon

3 eggs, separated

150 ml (5 fl oz) double cream, lightly whipped

For the base:

75 g (3 oz) digestive biscuits

40 g (1½ oz) butter

25 g (1 oz) demerara sugar

For the topping:

150 ml (5 fl oz) double cream, lightly whipped

450 g (1 lb) mixed blueberries and summer fruits (such as raspberries and small strawberries)

a little icing sugar for dusting (optional)

1 Lightly grease the cake tin. Cut a strip of non-stick baking parchment to fit around the sides of the tin, fold the bottom edge of the strip up by about 2.5 cm (1 in), creasing it firmly, then open out the fold and cut slanting lines into this narrow strip at intervals. Fit this into the greased tin with the snipped edge in the base of the tin and put a circle of non-stick baking parchment on top. For the base, put the digestive biscuits into a polythene bag and crush them to crumbs with a rolling pin. Melt the butter in a pan, add the crushed biscuits and demerara sugar and mix well.

2 Spread the crumb mixture over the base of the tin and press firmly with the back of a metal spoon. Leave in a cool place to set while you are mixing the cheesecake.

3 Pre-heat the oven to 160°C/
325°F/Gas Mark 3. Put the
butter, sugar, curd cheese,
flour, lemon zest and juice and
egg yolks into a large bowl
and beat well with a wooden
spoon or electric mixer until
smooth. Fold the lightly
whipped double cream into
the mixture using a plastic
spatula or large metal spoon.

6 Spread the lightly whipped
cream in the dip of the
cheesecake and scatter the
fruit haphazardly on top.
Lightly dust with icing sugar
if wished.

4 Put the egg whites into a
large bowl and whisk them
with a hand-held electric
mixer until stiff but not dry.
Fold them into the cheese
mixture.

5 Pour on to the biscuit base
and gently level the surface
with a plastic spatula. Bake
for about 1–1½ hours, until
set. Turn off the oven and
leave the cheesecake inside
for a further hour to cool. Run

a small palette knife around
the edge of the tin to loosen
the cheesecake, then push
the base up through the cake
tin. Remove the side paper
and put the cheesecake on to
a serving plate.

French apple tart

This classic tart is time-consuming to make but well worth the effort for a special occasion.

preparation time: 45 minutes
cooking time: 1–1¼ hours
tin needed: a loose-bottomed
    23 cm (9 in) fluted flan tin

50 g (2 oz) butter

900 g (2 lb) cooking apples, quartered, cored and cut into chunks (no need to peel)

2 tablespoons water

4 tablespoons apricot jam

50 g (2 oz) caster sugar

grated zest of ½ lemon

For the pastry:

175 g (6 oz) plain flour

15 g (½ oz) icing sugar

75 g (3 oz) butter, diced

1 egg yolk

about 1 tablespoon water

For the topping:

225 g (8 oz) eating apples

1–2 tablespoons lemon juice

about 1 teaspoon caster sugar

For the glaze:

4 tablespoons apricot jam

1 First make the pastry. Put the flour and icing sugar into a large bowl and rub in the butter with your fingertips until the mixture resembles fine breadcrumbs.

2 Add the egg yolk and water and mix until it comes together to form a firm dough. (This may, of course, all be done in a food processor.) Wrap in cling film and leave to rest in the fridge for about 30 minutes.

3 While the pastry is resting, pre-heat the oven to 200°C/400°F/Gas Mark 6 and make the filling. Melt the butter in a large pan and then add the apples and water. Cover and cook very gently for about 10–15 minutes, until the apples have become soft and mushy.

4 Rub the apples through a nylon sieve into a clean pan and add the apricot jam, sugar and grated lemon zest. Cook over a high heat for 10–15 minutes, stirring constantly, until all the excess liquid has evaporated and the apple purée is thick. (The mixture 'spits' as it thickens, and is very hot, so take care not to burn your arm.) Remove from the heat and leave to cool.

5 Roll out the pastry on a lightly floured work surface and use to line the flan tin. Prick the pastry all over with a fork, line with non-stick baking parchment or foil, fill with baking beans and bake blind for about 15 minutes. Remove the baking beans and paper and return the pastry case to the oven for 5 minutes or until it is pale golden and dried out. Remove from the oven but leave the oven turned on.

6 Spoon the cooled apple purée into the flan case and level the surface. Peel, quarter and core the eating apples, then slice them very thinly. Arrange in neat overlapping circles over the apple purée, brush with lemon juice and sprinkle with the caster sugar. Return the flan to the oven and bake for about 25 minutes, until the pastry and the edges of the apples are lightly browned. Allow to cool a little.

7 For the glaze, sieve the apricot jam into a small pan and heat gently until runny. Brush it over the top of the apples and the pastry. Serve warm or cold.

Cakes for Occasions

One of the great joys of baking is the satisfaction one gets from the 'ooh's and 'aah's when the finished cake is produced. There really is nothing better than the smell of freshly baked cakes and biscuits wafting from the kitchen, tempting everyone to come and try what's on offer and hardly being able to wait for it to cool before eating.

Whatever the occasion, choose something that you have time to make. The preparation times given throughout this book are approximate, and assume that you will be using a free-standing or hand-held mixer. If you are making by hand, the time will be a little longer. Check that you have all the ingredients ready before starting out and suitable tins where needed.

Below I give a few ideas for different occasions, but of course you can try whichever cakes you like.

Children's Tea Party

One of the secrets of success with the young, I find, is to make things small to tempt them – even éclairs can be made bite-sized. But ensure you have plenty of paper napkins and kitchen towels to hand for faces, hands and carpet!

Flapjacks

Mini St Clements Muffins

Chocolate Eclairs

Chocolate Crispies

Meringues

Cakes for Bazaars and Coffee Mornings

Presentation is very important when getting cakes ready to sell at these events. If the cakes are whole, they look smart when wrapped carefully in cellophane (rather than plastic); make sure you label them clearly. If they are made with butter, fresh lemon or real chocolate, it is quite a selling point to mention the fact. Remember that not everyone has a large family and a couple of pieces of cake, a few brownies or four or six biscuits on a paper plate are very inviting to buy and take home for tea.

Ginger and Treacle Spiced Traybake

Chocolate Brownies

Victoria Sandwich

Cakes That Keep Well

Many cakes keep well but take care either to wrap them carefully or to keep them in a tin or polythene box so that they don't dry out. Any cakes containing fresh cream should be kept in the fridge wrapped in cling film. Some cakes really improve with keeping, such as Sticky Gingerbread and Celebration Cake. Lemon drizzle cake never keeps long in our house, however, as it is such a favourite that no one can resist it!

Classic Sticky Gingerbread

Celebration Cake

Lemon Drizzle Traybake

Winter Desserts

These are four of my favourite winter puds. The roulade can be made ahead and frozen; once thawed, sprinkle generously with icing sugar before serving. For all age groups, Banoffi Pie is a real winner. The strudel is easy and lovely on a cold day. The Austrian Sachertorte is very rich and takes time to prepare, so it's perfect for a special occasion. It keeps well, so don't worry about any leftover slices.

The Ultimate Chocolate Roulade

Banoffi Pie

Spiced Apple Strudel

Sachertorte

Summer Desserts

Three of these are packed with fruit, which is a sign of summer – make the most of fresh fruits when they are in season and at their very best. The unfilled Pavlova and the finished roulade freeze well – meringue puddings always look spectacular.

Lemon Meringue Roulade

Blueberry and Summer Fruit Cheesecake

French Apple Tart

Pavlova

Kitchen Equipment Suppliers

Divertimenti
139–141 Fulham Road
London
SW3 6SD
Tel: 020 7581 8065
www.divertimenti.co.uk

Lakeland Ltd
Alexandra Buildings
Windermere
Cumbria
LA23 1BQ
Tel: 01539 488100
www.lakelandlimited.co.uk

Lift Off Paper (non-stick paper)
NKS
Dogcraig House
Peebles
Scotland
EH45 9HS
Tel/fax: 01721 729824
www.cooks-kitchen-equipment.co.uk

Magimix
19 Bridge Street
Godalming
Surrey
GU7 1HY
Tel: 01483 427411
www.magimix.com

Acknowledgements

I have been extremely fortunate to have Fiona Oysten to help me with this book. She has tested all the recipes with great professionalism (as she did with *Ultimate Cakes*). Tommy and Charlie, Fiona's children, are great tasters and have been thrilled that Mum was helping with this book. Thank you, Fiona.

As always, I thank Lucy Young, my assistant, by my side for fourteen years – full of new ideas, keeping me young and trendy and making me laugh day in, day out. Thank you, Lucy, for all your support and friendship.

Thank you, too, to Nicky Ross from BBC Books for asking me to write this book – lovely to work with you again. Also many thanks to Sarah Lavelle, Lisa Pettibone and Jane Middleton for their dedication and for making sure all the text and page layout is just perfect.

Index